SHIPS

OF WORLD WAR II

SHIPS
OF WORLD WAR II

John Ward

MBI Publishing Company

This edition first published in 2000 by MBI Publishing Company, 729 Prospect Avenue, PO Box 1, Osceola, WI 54020-0001 USA

MBI Publishing Company books are also available at discounts in bulk quantity for industrial or sales-promotional use. For details write to Special Sales Manager at Motorbooks International Wholesalers & Distributors, 729 Prospect Avenue, PO Box 1, Osceola, WI 54020-0001 USA.

Library of Congress Cataloging-in-Publication Data Available.

ISBN 0-7603-0935-3

Printed in Hong Kong

Editorial and design
Brown Partworks Limited
8 Chapel Place
Rivington Street
London
EC2A 3DQ
UK

Editor: Chris Westhorp
Picture research: Antony Shaw
Design: Spencer Holbrook
Production: Matt Weyland

Picture Credits
All photographs The Robert Hunt Library

CONTENTS

DUNKERQUE

SPECIFICATIONS

DUNKERQUE

Type: **Battleship**	Armour (deck): **139.7mm (5.5in)**
Length: **214.5m (703.75ft)**	Armour (turrets): **355.26mm (13.2in)**
Beam: **31.16m (102.25ft)**	Guns: **8x13in; 16x5.1in**
Draught: **8.68m (28.5ft)**	AA guns: **8x37mm; 32x13.2mm**
Displacement (normal): **26,924tnes (26,500t)**	Aircraft: **Two**
Displacement (full load): **36,068tnes (35,500t)**	Crew: **1431**
Machinery: **Steam Turbines**	Launched: **October 1935**
Armour (belt): **241.3mm (9.5in)**	Speed: **30 knots**

Launched on 2 October 1935 and completed in April 1937, *Dunkerque* was one of two new fast battleships on the French Navy's inventory in 1939, the other being the *Strasbourg*. At the outbreak of World War II in September 1939, these two vessels were the spearhead of a fast raiding force based at Brest, the battleships being supported by seven heavy cruisers, three light cruisers and some 50 destroyers.

This raiding force could achieve a speed of 30 knots, which at that time was not matched by any other naval force in the world. Dunkerque and her sister were modelled on the British "Nelson Class" and were fitted with a main armament of eight 330mm (13in) guns in two quadruple turrets.

On 3 July 1940, *Dunkerque* was moored in the Roads of Mers-el-Kebir and had begun to disarm, in accordance with the terms of the Armistice agreed between the Germans and the government of France, when she was attacked and severely damaged by British warships lying offshore. Three days later, she was further damaged during an attack by Royal Navy torpedo aircraft and partially sunk. After being refloated, she sailed for Toulon on 20 February 1942, and was scuttled there on 27 November that year when German forces occupied the port.

JEANNE D'ARC

The light cruiser *Jeanne D'Arc* was launched in February 1930 and completed in September 1931. The Armistice of June 1940 between the victorious Germans and the government of France found her in Martinique, where she was immobilized and disarmed on 1 May 1942 under the terms of an agreement signed between Admiral Robert, Governor of the island, and the US Government. The aircraft carrier *Bearn* and the light cruiser *Emile Bertin* were also decommissioned at this time. On 3 June 1943, Admiral Robert, who had remained loyal to the Vichy Government, turned Martinique over to the Free French Government in Algeria and made all three vessels available for war operations on the side of the Allies, providing much-needed firepower.

After refitting, during which her torpedo tubes were removed and her light armament modernised, *Jeanne D'Arc* took part in operations off Corsica and later formed part of the naval task force which shelled enemy positions along the Italian Riviera. She also carried out many transport operations, ferrying French troops and equipment from North Africa to the French Riviera after the Allied landings there in August 1944. *Jeanne D'Arc* served as a training ship postwar and remained on the French Navy's inventory until 1964.

SPECIFICATIONS

JEANNE D'ARC

Type: **Light Cruiser**	Armour (deck): **76mm (3in)**
Length: **170m (557.6ft)**	Armour (turrets): **95mm (3.75in)**
Beam: **17.5m (57.4ft)**	Guns: **8x155mm; 4x75mm**
Draught: **6.3m (20.6ft)**	AA guns: **4x37mm; 12x13.2mm**
Displacement (normal): **6600tnes (6496t)**	Aircraft: **One**
Displacement (full load): **9094tnes (8950t)**	Crew: **505**
Machinery: **Geared Turbines**	Launched: **February 1930**
Armour (belt): **120mm (4.75in)**	Speed: **25 knots**

MONTCALM

SPECIFICATIONS

MONTCALM

Type: **Light Cruiser**	Armour (deck): **50.8mm (2in)**
Length: **179m (587ft)**	Armour (turrets): **130mm (5in)**
Beam: **17.48m (57.3ft)**	Guns: **9x152mm**
Draught: **5.28m (17.3ft)**	AA guns: **8x90mm; 8x13.2mm**
Displacement (normal): **8342tnes (8214t)**	Aircraft: **Two**
Displacement (full load): **9266tnes (9120t)**	Crew: **540**
Machinery: **Boilers & Turbines**	Launched: **October 1935**
Armour (belt): **120mm (4.7in)**	Speed: **31 knots**

Launched in October 1935 and completed in December 1937, *Montcalm* was one of six light cruisers of the "La Galissonniere" class. The ships were very well designed and mounted an excellent main armament of nine 152mm (6in) guns. They were among the best in the French Navy, which was a world leader in military ships, at the outbreak of World War II in September 1939.

On 9 September 1940, *Montcalm*, accompanied by her sister ships *Marseillaise* and *Georges Leygues*, sailed from Toulon and reached Dakar, where they played their part in repulsing an unsuccessful attempt by British and Free French forces to take over the port on 23–25 September. In February 1943, after the French Command at Dakar joined the Allies, the three cruisers went to Philadelphia for a major refit, during which radar was installed and anti-aircraft armament increased.

On 6 June 1944, *Montcalm* and *Georges Leygues* formed part of the naval support force bombarding German shore positions at Omaha Beach during the invasion of Normandy, and in August they provided support for the Allied forces landing on the French Riviera. *Montcalm* and her sister vessels *Gloire* and *Georges Leygues* had active careers in the postwar French Navy; *Montcalm* herself was stricken in 1961.

RICHELIEU

The fast, modern battleship *Richelieu* was the leader of a class of three vessels, the others being the *Jean Bart* and *Clemenceau*. Launched in January 1939, the *Richelieu* escaped to Dakar in June 1940, and, on 8 July, she was damaged in a torpedo attack by British Fairey Swordfish carrier aircraft, her captain having refused demands to surrender or immobilize his ship. Despite being stranded in port, she used her 380mm (15in) guns to good advantage in beating off an attempt to capture Dakar by a combined Anglo/Free French force in September.

In January 1943, the French at Dakar having gone over to the Allies, she sailed for the United States to be repaired and refitted. In November 1943, she served briefly with the British Home Fleet before sailing for eastern waters in March 1944. On 25 July 1944, now serving with the British Eastern Fleet, she joined British warships in bombarding Sabang. From October 1944 to February 1945, she refitted at Casablanca, and in April 1945 she sailed for a second campaign with the Eastern Fleet.

After World War II she continued to serve the French Navy, and supported the French re-occupation of Indo-China in 1945-46. Placed in reserve in 1956, she was discarded in 1960 and broken up at the Italian port of La Spezia in 1968.

SPECIFICATIONS

RICHELIEU

Type: **Battleship**	*Armour (deck):* **170.18mm (6.7in)**
Length: **247.87 m (813.25ft)**	*Armour (turrets):* **429.26mm (16.9in)**
Beam: **33.14m (108.75ft)**	*Guns:* **8x15in; 9x6in; 12x3.9in**
Draught: **9.67m (31.75ft)**	*AA guns:* **16x37mm; 8x13.2mm**
Displacement (normal): **39,116tnes (38,500t)**	*Aircraft:* **Three**
Displacement (full load): **48,260tnes (47,500t)**	*Crew:* **1670**
Machinery: **Steam Turbines**	*Launched:* **January 1940**
Armour (belt): **345.44m (13.6in)**	*Speed:* **32 knots**

BISMARCK

SPECIFICATIONS

BISMARCK

Type:
Battleship

Length:
251m (823.5ft)

Beam:
35.96m (118ft)

Draught:
9.54m (31.3ft)

Displacement (normal):
46,923tnes (45,200t)

Displacement (full load):
51,763tnes (50,950t)

Machinery:
Steam Turbines

Armour (belt):
68mm (12.6in)

Armour (deck):
80mm (3.15in)

Armour (turrets):
360mm (14.2in)

Guns:
8x15in; 12x5.9in

AA guns:
14x4.1in; 16x37mm

Aircraft:
Six

Crew:
2100

Launched:
February 1939

Speed:
30 knots

Together with her sister ship, *Tirpitz*, the *Bismarck* was the pride of Hitler's navy, and was viewed with alarm by the Royal Navy. Launched in February 1939 and completed in August 1940, she underwent sea trials in the Baltic and in May 1941 she sailed in company with the heavy cruiser *Prinz Eugen* to attack Allied commerce in the Atlantic.

Detected by British aircraft, the German warships were intercepted by units of the British Home Fleet in the Denmark Strait, between Greenland and Iceland, and a running battle developed during which the *Bismarck* sank the battlecruiser HMS *Hood* and damaged the battleship *Prince of Wales*. Hits on the *Bismarck* reduced her speed, though, and produced an oil slick in her wake.

On 26 May she was attacked by Swordfish aircraft from the carrier *Ark Royal*; a torpedo hit destroyed her steering gear and rendered her unmanoeuvrable. On 27 May she was shelled to pieces by the battleships *King George V* and *Rodney*, her crew resisting until the last. Finished off by torpedoes and gunfire, she sank some 480km (300 miles) northwest of Brest with the loss of 1977 officers and men – a grievous loss to the German Navy. Half a century later, her wreck was photographed by a miniature submarine.

BLÜCHER

Launched in June 1937, the heavy cruiser *Blücher* was one of five vessels in her class, the others being the *Lützow, Seydlitz, Prinz Eugen* and *Admiral Hipper*. On 9 April 1940, flying the flag of Admiral Oskar Kummetz, she took part in the German invasion of Norway, leading a group of warships carrying 2000 troops and bound for the Norwegian capital, Oslo.

This spearhead force was to be followed by 15 transport vessels, carrying a further 3761 troops. Although the invasion – the first major amphibious operation of World War II — was meticulously well planned, Admiral Kummetz ordered his force to proceed through the Drobak Narrows, leading to Oslofjord, at only 12 knots. This would prove a costly decision for the German Navy. The waterway was only 457m (500yd) wide and was heavily defended by forts. Holding their fire until the Blücher was at point-blank range, the Norwegian gunners opened fire and quickly set her ablaze. Their torpedoes then reduced her to a helpless hulk, and at 06:30 hours she capsized and sank with the loss of over 1000 officers and men.

In the 1990s, fuel oil leaking from her corroded tanks began to pose a serious pollution threat, requiring a major underwater engineering effort in order to avert a large-scale environmental disaster.

SPECIFICATIONS

BLÜCHER

Type: **Heavy Cruiser**	Armour (deck): **50.8mm (2in)**
Length: **205.83m (675.3ft)**	Armour (turrets): **101.6mm (4in)**
Beam: **21.25m (69.75ft)**	Guns: **8x8in; 12x4.1in**
Draught: **5.79m (19ft)**	AA guns: **12x40mm; 8x37mm**
Displacement (normal): **14,474tnes (14,247t)**	Aircraft: **Three**
Displacement (full load): **18,499tnes (18,208t)**	Crew: **1600**
Machinery: **Boilers & Steam Turbines**	Launched: **June 1937**
Armour (belt): **76.2mm (3in)**	Speed: **32.5 knots**

EMDEN

SPECIFICATIONS

EMDEN

Type: **Light Cruiser**	Armour (deck): **38.1mm (1.5in)**
Length: **155m (508.75ft)**	Armour (conning tower): **101.6mm (4in)**
Beam: **14.32m (47ft)**	Guns: **8x5.9in; 3x3.5in**
Draught: **5.15m (16.9ft)**	AA guns: **2x40mm; 20x20mm**
Displacement (normal): **5780tnes (5689t)**	Aircraft: **None**
Displacement (full load): **7215tnes (7102t)**	Crew: **630**
Machinery: **Boilers & Steam Turbines**	Launched: **January 1925**
Armour (belt): **50.8mm (2in)**	Speed: **29 knots**

Completed in January 1925, the light cruiser *Emden* was the first medium-sized German warship built after World War I. Originally a coal-burning vessel, she was intended primarily for overseas service and consequently had a large bunker capacity; particular attention was paid to accommodation space and crew comfort, something of a novelty at that time. Her first mission in World War II was to lay mines in the North Sea, and, in April 1940, she was one of the warships that accompanied the *Blücher* during the invasion of Norway. Though this operation was a costly affair in terms in shipping, she survived and was later transferred to the Baltic and saw considerable operational service there, initially operating as part of a powerful task force that included the new battleship *Tirpitz* and later operating as a mine warfare training vessel.

In late 1944 and early 1945 she was involved in evacuating troops and civilians from East Prussia in the face of the Russian advance; one of her more unusual tasks, in January 1945, was to evacuate the coffin containing the body of Field Marshal von Hindenburg, which had been interred at the Tannenberg Memorial, from *Königsberg*. In April 1945 Emden was damaged in a bombing attack on Kiel. She was scuttled and broken up in 1949.

GNEISENAU

The battlecruiser *Gneisenau* was launched in December 1936 and completed in May 1938. She was upgraded in the following year and made her first Atlantic sortie, with her sister ship, *Scharnhorst,* in November 1939, sinking the British auxiliary cruiser *Rawalpindi.* She was damaged by gunfire from the British battlecruiser *Renown* off Norway on 9 April 1940, but on 8 June she and *Scharnhorst* sank the British aircraft carrier *Glorious* and her escorting destroyers *Ardent* and *Acasta.* On 20 June 1940 she was torpedoed by the Royal Navy submarine HMS *Clyde* off Trondheim. In January 1941, again with the *Scharnhorst,* she made another sortie into the Atlantic, the two sinking 22 merchant ships – a moderately successful action.

On 6 April 1941 she was torpedoed by a British aircraft at Brest, and further damaged by aircraft bombs four days later. In February 1942, with the *Scharnhorst* and the heavy cruiser *Prinz Eugen,* she made the famous dash through the English Channel from Brest to Germany, being damaged by a mine en route. On 27 February 1942 she was damaged by bombs at Kiel, after which her guns were removed and she was decommissioned. She was towed to Gdynia and sunk as a blockship there in March 1945. Her hulk was broken up in 1947–51.

SPECIFICATIONS

GNEISENAU

Type: **Battlecruiser**	Armour (deck): **50.8mm (2in)**
Length: **229.74m (753.75ft)**	Armour (turrets): **360.68mm (14.2in)**
Beam: **30m (98.3ft)**	Guns: **9x11in; 12x5.9in; 14x4in**
Draught: **8.68m (28.5ft)**	AA guns: **16x37mm; 8x20mm**
Displacement (normal): **35,407tnes (34,850t)**	Aircraft: **Three**
Displacement (full load): **39522tnes (38,900t)**	Crew: **1670**
Machinery: **Steam Turbines**	Launched: **December 1936**
Armour (belt): **350.5mm (13.8in)**	Speed: **31.5 knots**

GRAF SPEE

SPECIFICATIONS

GRAF SPEE

Type: Pocket Battleship	**Armour (deck):** 40.64mm (1.6in)
Length: 187.9m (616.5ft)	**Armour (turrets):** 139.7mm (5.5in)
Beam: 21.64m (71ft)	**Guns:** 6x11in; 8x5.9in; 6x3.5in
Draught: 7.31m (24ft)	**AA guns:** None
Displacement (normal): 13,818tnes (13,600t)	**Aircraft:** Two
Displacement (full load): 16,279tnes (16,023t)	**Crew:** 1150
Machinery: Diesel	**Launched:** June 1934
Armour (belt): 58.42mm (2.3in)	**Speed:** 26 knots

Officially classed as a Panzerschiff (Armoured Ship), but more popularly known as a "pocket battleship", the *Admiral Graf Spee* and her two sisters, the *Admiral Scheer* and *Deutschland*, were designed as commerce raiders with a large radius of action and complied with the restrictions imposed on Germany by the terms of the Treaty of Versailles (which was detested by the Nazi Party). The "pocket battleship" nickname derived from the fact that, although they were too small to be classed as battleships, they were more powerful and faster than most other warships then afloat. Their hulls were electrically welded, and armour protection was sacrificed to produce a higher speed.

The *Graf Spee* was launched in June 1934 and completed in January 1936. In 1936–37, during the Spanish Civil War, she was engaged in blockading Republican ports. Between September and November 1939, during a sortie into the South Atlantic, she sank or captured nine British merchant vessels before being brought to battle by a British naval force comprising the cruisers *Exeter, Ajax* and *Achilles* off the estuary of the River Plate. Forced to seek refuge in the neutral port of Montevideo, on 17 December she was scuttled; her captain, Hans Langsdorff, committed suicide rather than be taken prisoner.

KÖLN

Completed in May 1928, *Köln* was one of a class of three light cruisers in the German Navy, the others being the *Königsberg* and *Karlsruhe*. *Köln* was in action from the very first day of World War II, taking part in minelaying operations in the North Sea with Admiral Densch's Reconnaissance Force.

During the invasion of Norway in April 1940, she and the *Königsberg* formed part of the naval force covering the German landing at Bergen. *Köln* remained in northern waters until 1943, when she was transferred to the Baltic Fleet. She subsequently took part in many operations in support of German forces, and from late 1944, while serving with the Fleet Training Squadron, she was heavily involved in evacuating civilian and military personnel from East Prussia, a mission of some risk though one she performed very well.

On 30 March 1945, only a few weeks away from the end of the war, while undergoing a refit, she was badly damaged in a heavy attack on Wilhelmshaven Naval Dockyard by B-24 bombers of the United States Army Air Force (USAAF), settling on the bottom with only her superstructure above the surface. She was decommissioned on 6 April 1945, although her guns were still intact and she was used for local defence until the German surrender. She was scrapped in 1946.

SPECIFICATIONS

KÖLN

Type: **Light Cruiser**	Armour (deck): **38.1mm (1.5in)**
Length: **173.95m (570.75ft)**	Armour (turrets): **25.4mm (1in)**
Beam: **15.24m (50ft)**	Guns: **9x5.9in; 6x3.46in**
Draught: **5.58m (18.3ft)**	AA guns: **8x37mm**
Displacement (normal): **6864tnes (6756t)**	Aircraft: **Two**
Displacement (full load): **8392tnes (8260t)**	Crew: **820**
Machinery: **Boilers & Steam Turbines**	Launched: **May 1928**
Armour (belt): **68.58mm (2.7in)**	Speed: **32 knots**

LÜTZOW

SPECIFICATIONS

LÜTZOW

Type:
Pocket Battleship

Length:
187.9m (616.5ft)

Beam:
21.33m (70ft)

Draught:
7.23m (23.75ft)

Displacement (normal):
13,817tnes (13,600t)

Displacement (full load):
15,670tnes (15,423t)

Machinery:
Diesels

Armour (belt):
58.42mm (2.3in)

Armour (deck):
40.64mm (1.6in)

Armour (turrets):
139.7mm (5.5in)

Guns:
6x11in; 8x5.9in

AA guns:
6x3.46in

Aircraft:
Two

Crew:
1150

Launched:
May 1931

Speed:
26 knots

Originally named *Deutschland*, the *Lützow* was one of three armoured ships – the so-called "pocket battleships" – laid down between 1928 and 1931. *Deutschland* was the first of the class, being launched in May 1931 and completed in April 1933. She was originally used as a seagoing training ship, to familiarize crews with her new technology.

On 22 May 1937 she was damaged by bombs dropped by a Spanish Republican aircraft off Ibiza, 22 of her crew being killed. In October 1939, after the outbreak of World War II, she made a sortie into the Atlantic, sinking two merchant ships and capturing a third. On 15 November 1939 she was renamed Lützow, and in February 1940 she was reclassified as a heavy cruiser. During the invasion of Norway in April 1940 she was damaged by shore batteries and by a torpedo from the British submarine Spearfish.

On 13 June 1941 she was again badly damaged by a torpedo from a British aircraft off Norway. After repair, she remained in Norwegian waters in 1942–43 and then went to Gdynia for a refit, subsequently providing fire support for German forces in the Baltic area. On 16 April 1945 she was bombed and sunk by British aircraft, who were roaming the skies of Germany at will, in shallow water at Swinemunde.

PRINZ EUGEN

The *Prinz Eugen*, launched in August 1938, was the third of five heavy cruisers laid down for the Kriegsmarine in the 1930s. On 23 April 1941 she was damaged by a magnetic mine, but was repaired in time to sail for the Atlantic with the battleship *Bismarck* in May. *Prinz Eugen* managed to elude the British warships hunting the *Bismarck*, having been detached to make her own way to the French Atlantic ports, and so escaped *Bismarck*'s fate, arriving at Brest on 1 June 1941 undamaged. On 12 February 1942 she took part in the famous "Channel Dash" with the battlecruisers *Scharnhorst* and *Gneisenau*, which totally humiliated the Royal Navy.

She subsequently saw service in the Baltic with the Fleet Training Squadron, and in 1944 provided fire support to German forces resisting the Soviet advance. On 15 October 1944 she was badly damaged in collision with the light cruiser *Leipzig*.

The end of World War II found her at Copenhagen, where she surrendered to the Allies. She was allocated to the United States and was used as a target vessel in the atomic bomb tests at Bikini Atoll in 1946, which she survived in a badly damaged condition. Her hulk was finally sunk by American warships at Kwajalein on 15 November 1947.

SPECIFICATIONS

PRINZ EUGEN

Type: Heavy Cruiser	**Armour (deck):** 50.8mm (2in)
Length: 212.44m (697ft)	**Armour (turrets):** 101.6mm (4in)
Beam: 21.8m (71.5ft)	**Guns:** 8x8in; 12x4.1in
Draught: 7.16m (23.5ft)	**AA guns:** 12x40mm; 8x37mm
Displacement (normal): 14,500tnes (14,271t)	**Aircraft:** Three
Displacement (full load): 19,000tnes (18,700t)	**Crew:** 1600
Machinery: Boilers & Steam Turbines	**Launched:** August 1938
Armour (belt): 76.2mm (3in)	**Speed:** 33 knots

SCHARNHORST

SPECIFICATIONS

SCHARNHORST

Type: **Battlecruiser**	Armour (deck): **50.8mm (2in)**
Length: **230.96m (757.75ft)**	Armour (turrets): **360.68mm (14.2in)**
Beam: **30m (898.4ft)**	Guns: **9x11in; 12x5.9in; 14x4in**
Draught: **8.68m (28.5ft)**	AA guns: **16x37mm**
Displacement (normal): **35,408tnes (34,850t)**	Aircraft: **Three**
Displacement (full load): **39,522tnes (38,900t)**	Crew: **1670**
Machinery: **Steam Turbines**	Launched: **October 1936**
Armour (belt): **350.5mm (13.8in)**	Speed: **31.5 knots**

Laid down at Wilhelmshaven in April 1934 and launched in October 1936, the *Scharnhorst* and her sister ship *Gneisenau* were modelled on the uncompleted "Mackensen" class battlecruisers of World War I. Up until 1942 the pair operated as a single battle group, but after the "Channel Dash" of February that year – in which *Scharnhorst* was mined twice while en route from Brest to Kiel – she operated alone.

In January 1943, after repair, *Scharnhorst* was sent to Norway with the heavy cruiser *Prinz Eugen*, the two ships operating from Altenfjord together with the battleship *Tirpitz* and the heavy cruiser *Lützow*. In September 1943 *Scharnhorst* and *Tirpitz* bombarded shore installations on Spitzbergen, and on 25 December *Scharnhorst* sailed to intercept an Allied convoy (JW55B) heading from Scotland to Kola, in north Russia. However, the result was that she herself became the prey, for on the following day the German battlecruiser was intercepted off Norway's North Cape by a force of British cruisers and destroyers, which inflicted some damage on her after a brief action. Gunfire from the battleship *Duke of York* and torpedoes from the destroyers then reduced her to a blazing wreck. Even so, she fought on with her surviving armament until she finally blew up and sank that evening.

SCHLESWIG-HOLSTEIN

The *Schleswig-Holstein* was one of a class of five pre-dreadnought battleships, laid down in 1902–04. She was launched in December 1906, completed in July 1908 and subsequently served with the German High Seas Fleet, seeing action in the Battle of Jutland. In the last two years of the war she served in turn as a depot ship at Bremerhaven and an accommodation ship at Kiel, and was one of the small force of warships that Germany was permitted to retain by the Versailles Treaty for coastal defence in the post-war years.

After substantial reconstruction, she was used as a cadet training ship. In August 1939 she was brought back into firstline service to provide fire support for German forces invading Poland, and on 1 September her four 280mm (11in) guns fired the opening shots of World War II when she shelled the Polish fortress of Westerplatte (she was in the area on a goodwill visit. She continued the bombardment for a week, until the Polish garrison surrendered on 7 September.

She later led a battle group covering troop transports in the invasion of Norway in 1940, before returning to the Baltic to reassume her role as a training vessel. On 18 December 1944 she was severely damaged in an RAF bombing raid on Gdynia, and was finally scuttled on 21 March 1945.

SPECIFICATIONS

SCHLESWIG-HOLSTEIN

Type: **Pre-Dreadnought**	*Armour (deck):* **38.1mm (1.5in)**
Length: **127.55m (418.5ft)**	*Armour (turrets):* **279.4mm (11in)**
Beam: **22.12m (72.6ft)**	*Guns:* **4x11in; 14x6.7in; 20x3.5in**
Draught: **8.22m (27ft)**	*AA guns:* **None**
Displacement (normal): **13,400tnes (13,190t)**	*Aircraft:* **None**
Displacement (full load): **14,441tnes (14,220t)**	*Crew:* **745**
Machinery: **Boilers**	*Launched:* **December 1906**
Armour (belt): **228.6mm (9in)**	*Speed:* **18 knots**

TIRPITZ

SPECIFICATIONS

TIRPITZ

Type:
Battleship

Armour (deck):
80mm (3.15in)

Length:
251m (823.5ft)

Armour (turrets):
360.68mm (14.2in)

Beam:
36m (118ft)

Guns:
8x15in; 12x5.9in; 16x4.1in

Draught:
9.45m (31ft)

AA guns:
16x37mm

Displacement (normal):
45,923tnes (45,200t)

Aircraft:
Six

Displacement (full load):
51,765tnes (50,950t)

Crew:
2100

Machinery:
Steam Turbines

Launched:
April 1939

Armour (belt):
320mm (12.6in)

Speed:
30 knots

The mighty battleship *Tirpitz* was laid down in October 1936 and was originally known as *Schlachtschiff G* or *Ersatz Schleswig-Holstein* (Replacement Schleswig-Holstein). She was launched on 1 April 1939 and completed in February 1941.

From early 1942 she was based at various locations in Norway, and on 8 September 1943 she sailed from Altenfjord to bombard shore installations on Spitzbergen – the only time she fired her guns in anger against a surface target. On 22 September she was damaged in an attack by British midget submarines, and on 3 April 1944 she was further damaged in an attack by carrier aircraft of the British Fleet Air Arm, sustaining 14 bomb hits and suffering 122 dead. She was subjected to further attacks by the Fleet Air Arm in August 1944, but sustained only minor bomb hits.

On 15 September 1944, however, she was attacked by RAF Lancasters while at anchor in Tromsö and was damaged by one of the RAF's new 5443kg (12,000lb) "Tallboy" deep penetration bombs. She was now no longer seaworthy, but on 12 November 1944 she was again attacked by Lancasters carrying 'Tallboy" bombs and received two direct hits, capsizing with the loss of 902 officers and men. Her hulk was gradually cut up over the next 12 years.

ARGONAUT

Built by Cammell Laird and launched in September 1941, HMS *Argonaut* was one of 16 "Dido"-class light cruisers completed for the British Royal Navy between 1939 and 1942.

After service with the Home Fleet, she was transferred to Gibraltar for service with Force H and took part in Operation Torch, the Allied landings in North Africa in November 1942. After refitting in the United States in 1943, she returned to the Home Fleet in time to participate in the Normandy landings on 6 June 1944, forming part of the maritime support force for the landing on "Gold" Beach, and in August she lent fire support during the Allied landings on the French Riviera. In September-October 1944 she formed part of the naval force covering Allied landings in Greece and the Aegean Islands, after which she sailed to join the Eastern Fleet in Ceylon.

In December 1944 and January 1945 she covered British carrier task forces attacking targets in Sumatra, after which she deployed to the Pacific as part of the British Pacific Fleet. She remained operational in the Pacific for the rest of the war, covering the British Task Force 37 operating off Okinawa and the Japanese Home Islands. *Argonaut* was finally scrapped at Newport in November 1955.

SPECIFICATIONS

ARGONAUT

Type: **Light Cruiser**	Armour (deck): **50.8mm (2in)**
Length: **156m (512ft)**	Armour (turrets): **38.1mm (1.5in)**
Beam: **15.24m (50ft)**	Guns: **10x5.25in**
Draught: **5.18m (17ft)**	AA guns: **8x2pdr; 8x.5in**
Displacement (normal): **5933tnes (5840t)**	Aircraft: **None**
Displacement (full load): **7193tnes (7080t)**	Crew: **487**
Machinery: **Steam Turbines**	Launched: **September 1941**
Armour (belt): **38.1mm (1.5in)**	Speed: **31.75 knots**

AJAX

SPECIFICATIONS

AJAX

Type: **Light Cruiser**	Armour (deck): **50.8mm (2in)**
Length: **168.85m (554ft)**	Armour (turrets): **25.4mm (1in)**
Beam: **16.76m (55ft)**	Guns: **8x6in; 4x4in**
Draught: **6.03m (19.8ft)**	AA guns: **12x.5in**
Displacement (normal): **7549tnes (7430t)**	Aircraft: **One**
Displacement (full load): **9500tnes (9350t)**	Crew: **570**
Machinery: **Steam Turbines**	Launched: **September 1932**
Armour (belt): **88.9mm (3.5in)**	Speed: **32.5 knots**

A "Leander"-class light cruiser, built by Vickers-Armstrong and launched in March 1934, HMS *Ajax* was in the South Atlantic on anti-commerce raider duty in the weeks following the outbreak of World War II in September 1939. In December 1939, together with the cruisers *Exeter* and *Achilles*, she intercepted and engaged the German pocket battleship *Admiral Graf Spee* off the estuary of the River Plate, being severely damaged in the action (the action was made famous in the film *The Battle of the River Plate*). After substantial repairs, she deployed to the Mediterranean, where she took part in convoy escort duty.

On 28 May 1941 she was damaged by German dive-bombers while en route to take part in the evacuation of British and Greek forces from the island of Crete, and was again damaged by air attack off the Algerian coast in January 1943. At the D-Day landings, the invasion of Normandy, in June 1944, she joined the cruisers *Argonaut*, *Orion* and *Emerald* in providing fire support for the assault on "Gold" Beach; she also covered the Allied landings in southern France in August.

In September-October 1944 she operated in the Aegean. She remained with the Mediterranean Fleet for the remainder of the war and was scrapped in November 1949.

ARK ROYAL

Laid down at the Cammell Laird Shipyard in September 1934, the aircraft carrier *Ark Royal* combined the best features of previous designs, incorporating a full-length flight deck overhanging the stern. Launched on 13 April 1937 and completed in November 1938, she was employed in the search for German vessels attempting to reach their home ports at the outbreak of World War II, during which operations she narrowly escaped being torpedoed by a U-boat.

In April 1940 her aircraft provided cover for Allied forces during the evacuation of Norway. In July 1940 her aircraft carried out attacks on French warships at Mers-el-Kebir, and later in the year she carried out convoy protection duty in the Mediterranean. In May 1941 she took part in the hunt for the *Bismarck*, her Swordfish aircraft achieving torpedo hits that sent the warship out of control and directly led to her destruction.

In the following months, on several occasions, she flew off reinforcement aircraft for the besieged island of Malta. These were dangerous missions, as Axis aircraft and submarines were very active at this time. It was after one such operation, as she was heading back to Gibraltar on 13 November 1941, that she was hit by the submarine *U81*. She sank under tow the next day, for the loss of only one life.

SPECIFICATIONS

ARK ROYAL

Type: Aircraft Carrier	**Armour (deck):** 88.9mm (3.5in)
Length: 243.84m (800ft)	**Armour (turrets):** N/A
Beam: 28.65m (94ft)	**Guns:** 16x4.5in
Draught: 8.53m (28ft)	**AA guns:** 32x2pdr; 32x.5in
Displacement (normal): 23,978tnes (23,600t)	**Aircraft:** 60
Displacement (full load): 28,936tnes (28,480t)	**Crew:** 1600
Machinery: Steam Turbines	**Launched:** April 1937
Armour (belt): 24.3mm (4.5in)	**Speed:** 32 knots

AUDACITY

SPECIFICATIONS

AUDACITY

Type: **Escort Carrier**	Armour (deck): **None**
Length: **142.3m (467ft)**	Armour (turrets): **N/A**
Beam: **17.06m (56ft)**	Guns: **1x4in**
Draught: **8.38m (27.5ft)**	AA guns: **6x20mm**
Displacement (normal): **Unknown**	Aircraft: **Eight**
Displacement (full load): **11,172tnes (11,000t)**	Crew: **650**
Machinery: **Diesel Turbines**	Launched: **March 1939**
Armour (belt): **None**	Speed: **16 knots**

HMS *Audacity*, the Royal Navy's first escort carrier, was a conversion of the German merchant vessel *Hannover*, captured in the West Indies in February 1940. Conversion was completed in June 1941, and from September she was used on the UK-Gibraltar route, her American-built Grumman Martlet fighters proving of great value in scouting for enemy submarines and fighting off the Focke-Wulf Condor maritime reconnaissance aircraft which, in the first half of 1941, had sunk a greater tonnage of Allied shipping than any other Axis aircraft or vessel, including the deadly U-boats. One of *Audacity*'s Martlets actually shot down a Condor on 21 September, during the carrier's first operational voyage.

During her final voyage, which began on 14 December 1941, no fewer than four Condors were destroyed by the carrier's Martlets, and her Swordfish made attacks on enemy U-boats, one of which, the *U131*, was unable to submerge as a result and had to be scuttled when British warships approached. However, on the night of 22–23 December *Audacity* was torpedoed and sunk by the *U751*. She was the forerunner of many escort carriers, which were to contribute greatly to the defeat of the U-boats during the strategically vital Battle of the Atlantic.

BARHAM

HMS *Barham* was one of five fast battleships of the "Queen Elizabeth" class, laid down in 1912–13 to replace battlecruisers as the offensive element of the battle fleet.

Launched in December 1914 and completed in October 1915, *Barham* served with the Grand Fleet throughout World War I and saw action at Jutland, where she received six hits. Reconstructed in 1927–28, she served in the Mediterranean until 1939, when she was assigned to the Home Fleet. On 12 December 1939 she sank the destroyer *Duchess* in a collision off the west coast of Scotland. Her bad luck continued to dog her, as a fortnight later she was damaged by a torpedo from the *U30* off the Clyde estuary.

Reassigned to the Mediterranean Fleet after repair, she was damaged by gunfire from the French battleship *Richelieu* during the Anglo-French attack on Dakar, and was again damaged by air attack off Crete on 27 May 1941, during the German airborne invasion of the island. She took part in several shore bombardment operations, her 381mm (15in) guns being used to good effect against enemy installations at Bardia, Libya. On 25 November 1941 she was torpedoed three times by the *U331*, capsized and blew up off Sollum, Egypt, with the loss of 862 lives.

SPECIFICATIONS

BARHAM

Type: **Battleship**	Armour (deck): **76.2mm (3in)**
Length: **196m (643ft)**	Armour (turrets): **330.2mm (13in)**
Beam: **31.7m (104ft)**	Guns: **8x15in; 4x6in**
Draught: **10.41m (34.1ft)**	AA guns: **2x4in**
Displacement (normal): **29,616tnes (29,150t)**	Aircraft: **2–3**
Displacement (full load): **33,528tnes (33,000t)**	Crew: **1297**
Machinery: **Steam Turbines**	Launched: **December 1914**
Armour (belt): **330.2mm (13in)**	Speed: **25 knots**

BELFAST

SPECIFICATIONS

BELFAST

Type:
Heavy Cruiser

Length:
186.8m (613ft)

Beam:
19.2m (63ft)

Draught:
6m (20ft)

Displacement (normal):
10,805tnes (10,635t)

Displacement (full load):
13,386tnes (13,175t)

Machinery:
Steam Turbines

Armour (belt):
123.9mm (4.88in)

Armour (deck):
76.2mm (3in)

Armour (turrets):
101.6mm (4in)

Guns:
12x6in; 12x4in

AA guns:
16x2pdr; 8x.5in

Aircraft:
Three

Crew:
780

Launched:
March 1938

Speed:
33 knots

The cruiser HMS *Belfast* and her sister ship, *Edinburgh*, were both laid down in December 1936 and launched in March 1938. *Belfast* was the larger of the two; in fact, she was the largest cruiser ever built for the Royal Navy.

Belfast suffered an early misfortune when, in November 1939, she was badly damaged by a magnetic mine, which exploded beneath the forward engine room, breaking her back and fracturing all the machinery mountings. She returned to service in October 1942, having undergone a number of modifications, and was assigned to Arctic convoy escort duty. In December 1943 she took part in the Battle of North Cape, which culminated in the destruction of the German Navy battlecruiser *Scharnhorst*.

On 6 June 1944 she formed part of the naval force assigned to support the Allied landing on "Juno" Beach in Normandy, and on the 26th she joined other warships in bombarding German positions in the Caen area. *Belfast* continued to serve for many years postwar; she was refitted in 1963 and placed in reserve, being designated a headquarters ship in 1966. In 1971 she was preserved as a permanent memorial, being moored at Simon's Wharf on the River Thames. She continues to be a popular tourist attraction.

CENTURION

HMS *Centurion* was a dreadnought of the 1910 "King George V" class. She was laid down at Devonport in January 1911 and launched in November of that year. On 9 December 1912 she sank the Italian steamer *Derna* in a collision while on her sea trials. Completed in May 1913, she served with the Grand Fleet for the duration of World War I and saw action at the indecisive Battle of Jutland in 1916.

From 1919 to 1924 she served in the Mediterranean and the Black Sea, after which she was converted as a remotely-controlled target ship.

In 1939–40 she underwent another conversion, being modified to resemble the battleship HMS *Anson*. She retained this role until 1942, being transferred to Alexandria, and in June 1942 she made an operational sortie as part of a force running supplies through to Alexandria to Malta (Operation Vigorous). By this stage of her career, though, she was rather obsolete and very vulnerable to air attack.

She subsequently served as a floating anti-aircraft battery, being anchored south of Suez. Reduced to Care and Maintenance status, she made her last voyage in June 1944, proceeding to the English Channel to be sunk off Normandy on 9 June to form a breakwater as part of an artificial harbour.

SPECIFICATIONS

CENTURION

Type: **Battleship**	Armour (deck): **102mm (4in)**
Length: **181.2m (597.6ft)**	Armour (turrets): **279mm (11in)**
Beam: **27.1m (89ft)**	Guns: **10x343mm**
Draught: **8.7m (28.75ft)**	AA guns: **4x102mm**
Displacement (normal): **23,369tnes (23,000t)**	Aircraft: **None**
Displacement (full load): **26,112tnes (25,700t)**	Crew: **782**
Machinery: **Four Turbines**	Launched: **November 1911**
Armour (belt): **305mm (12in)**	Speed: **21.75 knots**

DUKE OF YORK

SPECIFICATIONS

DUKE OF YORK

Type: Battleship	**Armour (deck):** 152.4mm (6in)
Length: 227m (745ft)	**Armour (turrets):** 330.2mm (13in)
Beam: 31.39m (103ft)	**Guns:** 10x14in; 15x5.25in
Draught: 9.6m (31.5ft)	**AA guns:** 64x2pdr
Displacement (normal): 38,608tnes (38,000t)	**Aircraft:** Two
Displacement (full load): 45,517tnes (44,800t)	**Crew:** 1900
Machinery: Steam Turbines	**Launched:** February 1940
Armour (belt): 381mm (15in)	**Speed:** 29 knots

One of five battleships that formed the 1936 "King George V" class, the *Duke of York* – originally laid down as the *Anson* and renamed in 1938 – was launched in February 1940 and completed in November 1941, a month before her sister ship, *Prince of Wales*, was sunk by Japanese air attack off Malaya.

One of the new battleship's first tasks was to carry the British Prime Minister, Winston Churchill, across the Atlantic for a meeting with US President Franklin D. Roosevelt in December 1941. From 1942 she was employed primarily on convoy protection duties in Atlantic and Arctic waters during the Battle of the Atlantic, but in November 1942 she joined the battleships *Nelson* and *Rodney* in providing fire support for the Allied landings in North Africa.

In December 1943 her gunfire was instrumental in the destruction of the German battlecruiser *Scharnhorst* off North Cape, the enemy warship being finished off by torpedo attacks. In 1945, after a refit, she sailed to join the British Pacific Fleet, arriving in August, too late to participate in the hostilities (where she would have provided support for the invasion of the Japanese home lands). In November 1951 the *Duke of York* was laid up in reserve, and in 1958 she was broken up at Faslane, Scotland.

DUNEDIN

HMS *Dunedin* was one of a class of eight light cruisers launched at the close of, or just after, World War I. Most served in the Far East, the South Atlantic or the Mediterranean. *Dunedin* herself was launched on 19 November 1918 and was loaned to the Royal New Zealand Navy between 1924 and 1937, along with a sister ship, *Diomede.*

Reassigned to the Royal Navy before the outbreak of World War II, she formed part of the Northern Patrol from 6 September 1939, searching for enemy vessels attempting to reach Germany. In 1940 she was assigned to convoy escort duty, and in June 1941 she captured the German supply ship *Lothringen*, stationed in the Atlantic to replenish U-boats operating off Freetown, Sierra Leone. In the weeks that followed she captured two Vichy French steamers.

On 24 November, 1941, she was searching for U-boats sent to assist the German commerce raider *Atlantis* when she was sighted by the German submarine *U124* (commanded by)Lt Cdr Mohr) which torpedoed and sank her. She was the only one of her class to be lost through enemy action in World War II; the others were scrapped after the war with the exception of HMS *Dragon*, sunk as a breakwater off Normandy to form part of an artificial harbour.

SPECIFICATIONS

DUNEDIN

Type: **Light Cruiser**	Armour (deck): **25.4mm (1in)**
Length: **143.86m (472ft)**	Armour (turrets): **25.4mm (1in)**
Beam: **14m (46ft)**	Guns: **6x6in; 2x3in**
Draught: **4.87m (16ft)**	AA guns: **2x2pdr**
Displacement (normal): **4663tnes (4590t)**	Aircraft: **None**
Displacement (full load): **5811tnes (5720t)**	Crew: **450**
Machinery: **Steam Turbines**	Launched: **November 1918**
Armour (belt): **76.2mm (3in)**	Speed: **30 knots**

EDINBURGH

SPECIFICATIONS

EDINBURGH

Type: **Cruiser**	Armour (deck): **76.2mm (3in)**	
Length: **18.7m (613ft)**	Armour (turrets): **101.6mm (4in)**	
Beam: **19.2m (63ft)**	Guns: **12x6in; 12x4in**	
Draught: **8.83m (29ft)**	AA guns: **16x2pdr; 8x.5in**	
Displacement (normal): **10,805tnes (10,635t)**	Aircraft: **Three**	
Displacement (full load): **13,386tnes (13,175t)**	Crew: **780**	
Machinery: **Steam Turbines**	Launched: **March 1938**	
Armour (belt): **124mm (4.88in)**	Speed: **33 knots**	

The cruiser HMS *Edinburgh* was launched on 31 March 1938, a fortnight after her sister ship, HMS *Belfast*. Both vessels spent the early weeks of World War II searching for German blockade runners, heading homewards via the Norwegian Sea.

In 1940 her main role was convoy protection, but in 1941 she made an occasional foray into the Arctic to hunt down German weather observation ships. In May 1941 she took part in the hunt for the German battleship *Bismarck*, and in July she was deployed to the Mediterranean for convoy escort duty, remaining with the 18th Cruiser Squadron at Gibraltar for several months.

The early weeks of 1942 saw *Edinburgh* assigned to the protection of convoys sailing the Arctic route to Russia. This was a dangerous task, and it was while she was engaged in this work, on 30 April, that she was hit and disabled by two torpedoes from the *U456* (Lt Cdr Teichert). Despite this, she succeeded in inflicting severe damage on the destroyer *Hermann Schoemann*, one of a force of enemy ships sent out to attack her. One of these ships, however, hit the *Edinburgh* with another torpedo with the result that she had to be abandoned and later sunk by a torpedo from the British destroyer *Foresight* on 2 May 1942.

FORMIDABLE

The Fleet Carrier HMS *Formidable* was one of four laid down in 1937, the others being the *Illustrious*, *Indomitable* and *Victorious*. All three had armoured flight decks, a feature that was to save them from disaster on several occasions. Launched in August 1939 and completed in November 1940, Formidable was deployed to the Mediterranean in March 1941 and was almost immediately in action, her aircraft achieving torpedo hits on the Italian battleship *Vittorio Veneto* and the cruiser *Pola* at the Battle of Cape Matapan (26–29 March 1941). This was a British victory and somewhat of a triumph for the Fleet Air Arm.

On 26 May 1941 she was badly damaged by German bombs off Crete. She underwent repairs at Norfolk, Virginia, and in 1943 was assigned to the Gibraltar-based Force H. Her aircraft provided cover for the Allied landings on Sicily and in Italy later in the year. In 1944 she was transferred to the Home Fleet, her aircraft taking part in attacks on the German battleship *Tirpitz*.

In 1945 she sailed for the Pacific Ocean and saw action off Okinawa, being twice damaged by *kamikazes* in May near the Japanese hom,e lands. On both occasions, though, her armoured flight deck preserved her from serious harm. Placed in reserve in 1948, she was broken up in 1953.

SPECIFICATIONS

FORMIDABLE

Type: **Fleet Carrier**	Armour (deck): **50.8mm (2in)**
Length: **225.55m (740ft)**	Armour (turrets): **N/A**
Beam: **28.96m (95ft)**	Guns: **16x4.5in**
Draught: **8.54m (28ft)**	AA guns: **42x2pdr**
Displacement (normal): **23,957tnes (23,580t)**	Aircraft: **36**
Displacement (full load): **29,078tnes (28,620t)**	Crew: **1230**
Machinery: **Steam Turbines**	Launched: **August 1939**
Armour (belt): **114.3mm (4.5in)**	Speed: **32 knots**

FURIOUS

SPECIFICATIONS

FURIOUS

Type: **Fleet Carrier**	Armour (deck): **50.8mm (2in)**
Length: **239.57m (786ft)**	Armour (turrets): **N/A**
Beam: **27.12m (89ft)**	Guns: **10x5.5in; 2x4in**
Draught: **8.23m (27ft)**	AA guns: **4x2pdr**
Displacement (normal): **23,165tnes (22,600t)**	Aircraft: **36**
Displacement (full load): **27,229tnes (26,800t)**	Crew: **1218**
Machinery: **Steam Turbines**	Launched: **August 1916**
Armour (belt): **76.2mm (3in)**	Speed: **31 knots**

Launched in August 1916 and completed in June 1917, HMS *Furious* was laid down as a light battlecruiser, being converted to the role of aircraft carrier by having a hangar and flight deck installed aft. Recommissioned in March 1915, she launched the first successful carrier-borne raid on 19 July 1918, her Sopwith Camel aircraft attacking the German Zeppelin base at Tondern and destroying two airships. Missions such as these proved the viability of aircraft operating from ships, and were a foretaste of things to come in World War II.

In 1921–25 she was fully converted as an aircraft carrier, having a complete flight deck fitted, and in 1939 a small island was added in the course of a refit. During the Norwegian campaign of 1940 she flew off reinforcement aircraft, an exercise successfully repeated in the Mediterranean a year later when she provided reinforcement fighters for Malta on several occasions.

After the German invasion of Russia in June 1941 she operated in Arctic waters, her aircraft attacking German-occupied Norwegian harbour installations, and in 1944 her air group took part in the attacks on the German battleship *Tirpitz*. Her active service over, the veteran carrier was placed in reserve later in the year. She was broken up in 1948.

HERMES

HMS *Hermes* was the first vessel designed from the outset as an aircraft carrier, having a small cruiser-type hull and engines, a full flight deck and large island. Launched on 11 September 1919 and completed in February 1924, she served in the Far East in the years between the two world wars, undergoing a refit in 1933. During her career she was to see much action.

At the outbreak of World War II she was in the South Atlantic, her aircraft being involved in the attack on Dakar in July 1940. She deployed to the East Indies soon afterwards, and in February 1941, on station in the Indian Ocean, she supported the British offensive against the Italians in Somaliland. In the following months she was involved in convoy protection in the Indian Ocean and South Atlantic.

Early in 1942 she was part of the Royal Navy's Eastern Fleet, based at Trincomalee, Ceylon. On 8 April 1942, air reconnaissance reported a Japanese carrier task force approaching the island of Ceylon and *Hermes* was ordered to put to sea, along with the Australian destroyer *Vampire*, the corvette *Hollyhock* and two tankers. The ships were attacked by some 80 Japanese aircraft, and all five were sunk. *Hermes* had no aircraft on board, and was defenceless, her anti-aircraft guns proving ineffective. Over 300 of her crew perished.

SPECIFICATIONS

HERMES

Type: **Fleet Carrier**	Armour (deck): **25.4mm (1in)**
Length: **182.88m (600ft)**	Armour (turrets): **N/A**
Beam: **21.41m (70.25ft)**	Guns: **6x5.5in**
Draught: **6.55m (21.5ft)**	AA guns: **3x4in; 6x20mm; 8x.5in**
Displacement (normal): **11,024tnes (10,850t)**	Aircraft: **20**
Displacement (full load): **13,208tnes (13,000t)**	Crew: **700**
Machinery: **Boilers & Steam Turbines**	Launched: **September 1919**
Armour (belt): **76.2mm (3in)**	Speed: **25 knots**

HOOD

SPECIFICATIONS

HOOD

Type: Battlecruiser	**Armour (deck):** 76.2mm (3in)
Length: 262.2m (860.5ft)	**Armour (turrets):** 279.4mm (11in)
Beam: 32m (105ft)	**Guns:** 8x15in
Draught: 10.14m (33.3ft)	**AA guns:** 14x4in; 24x2pdr; 8x.5in
Displacement (normal): 42,774tnes (42,100t)	**Aircraft:** None
Displacement (full load): 46,939tnes (46,200t)	**Crew:** 1421
Machinery: Boilers & Steam Turbines	**Launched:** August 1918
Armour (belt): 304.8mm (12in)	**Speed:** 28.8 knots

HMS *Hood* was designed as an enlarged version of the "Queen Elizabeth" class battlecruisers in response to the German "Mackensen" class. Launched on 22 August 1918 and completed in March 1920, she was the largest warship in the world, and remained so until World War II. With a speed of 32 knots she was also one of the fastest, deck armour having been sacrificed to produce a higher speed. Much was expected of this vessel in the interwar period.

In 1923–24 she undertook a much-publicized world cruise. Her first operational sortie of World War II was to form part of a blockade across the Iceland-Faeroes-UK gap. In July 1940 she was one of the British ships that bombarded the French harbour of Mers-el-Kebir. In the latter part of 1940 she underwent a refit, during which her spotter aircraft's catapult was removed and her AA armament increased.

In May 1941, together with the battleship *Prince of Wales*, *Hood* sailed to intercept the German battleship *Bismarck* and the heavy cruiser *Prinz Eugen* in the Denmark Strait. In the running battle that followed a salvo from the battleship *Bismarck* plummeted through *Hood*'s lightly-armoured deck and penetrated into a magazine. She blew up at once and sank with the loss of 1338 crew.

INDOMITABLE

A Fleet Carrier of the "Illustrious" class, HMS *Indomitable* was launched on 26 March 1940 and completed in October 1941. In November she went aground off Jamaica while working up, delaying her deployment to the Indian Ocean, where she was to provide the air component of the Eastern Fleet.

In May 1942 she joined her sister ship *Illustrious* in attacking the Vichy French garrison on Madagascar, and in July 1943 she provided air cover for the Sicily invasion force. During these operations she was damaged by an Italian torpedo.

In July 1944 she rejoined the Eastern Fleet, and together with the Royal Navy aircraft carrier *Illustrious*, began a series of attacks on enemy communications in Sumatra. In January 1945, she sailed from Trincomalee for Sydney, Australia, with the carriers *Illustrious*, *Indefatigable* and *Victorious* to form the nucleus of the British Pacific Fleet, and in April saw action off Okinawa, where she, like many ships, was damaged in a *kamikaze* attack. She was again damaged in May, during attacks on the Sakishima-Gunto island group. On her final mission of World War II she led the task force that reoccupied Hong Kong. She underwent a major refit after the war and was placed on the reserve list in 1953, being broken up in 1955.

SPECIFICATIONS

INDOMITABLE

Type: **Fleet Carrier**	Armour (deck): **76.2mm (3in)**
Length: **243.84m (800ft)**	Armour (turrets): **N/A**
Beam: **28.87m (94.75ft)**	Guns: **16x4.5in**
Draught: **8.45m (27.75ft)**	AA guns: **16x2pdr; 10x20mm**
Displacement (normal): **22,709tnes (22,352t)**	Aircraft: **55**
Displacement (full load): **28,593tnes (28,143t)**	Crew: **1600**
Machinery: **Boilers & Steam Turbines**	Launched: **March 1940**
Armour (belt): **101.6mm (4in)**	Speed: **31 knots**

KELLY

SPECIFICATIONS

KELLY

Type: **Destroyer**	Armour (deck): **12.7mm (.5in)**
Length: **108.66m (356.5ft)**	Armour (turrets): **12.7mm (.5in)**
Beam: **10.87m (35.75ft)**	Guns: **6x4.7in**
Draught: **2.74m (9ft)**	AA guns: **4x2pdr; 8x.5in**
Displacement (normal): **1722tnes (1695t)**	Aircraft: **None**
Displacement (full load): **2367tnes (2330t)**	Crew: **218**
Machinery: **Boilers & Steam Turbines**	Launched: **October 1938**
Armour (belt): **19mm (.75in)**	Speed: **36.5 knots**

Built by Hawthorn Leslie and launched on 25 October 1938, the "K"-class destroyer HMS *Kelly* was destined to become a famous ship with a famous captain – Lord Louis Mountbatten (the exploits of the ship and her captain were made famous in the film *In Which We Serve*, which painted a rather rosy view of life in the wartime Royal Navy). She was active in the closing stages of the Norwegian campaign, covering the evacuation of Allied troops from Namsos and other locations, and on 10 May 1940, during a sortie into the Skagerrak with six other destroyers and the cruiser *Birmingham*, she was badly damaged by a torpedo from the German MTB S31 and had to be towed to Newcastle-upon-Tyne by the destroyer *Bulldog*. After repair she deployed to the Mediterranean, in which all vessels of the "K" and "J" classes served and suffered heavy losses.

Early in May 1941 she was involved in convoy escort duty and also in shelling coastal targets, notably the harbour of Benghazi. The "K" class boats were not particularly well defended against air attack, a deficiency that was to have tragic consequences when Stuka dive-bombers sank both *Kelly* and her sister ship, *Kashmir*, off the island of Crete on 23 May 1941. Of the 17 "K" and "J" class boats that served in the Mediterranean, no fewer than 12 were lost through enemy action.

KING GEORGE V

The five "King George V" class battleships were laid down in 1936–37 as replacements for the Royal Sovereign class of 1913 vintage. Apart from *KGV* herself, the others were *Anson*, *Duke of York*, *Howe* and *Prince of Wales*, the latter destined to be sunk off Malaya in December 1941.

King George V was launched on 21 February 1939 and completed on 11 December 1940. Assigned to the Home Fleet, one of her first missions was to transport Prime Minister Churchill to the United States for a meeting with President Roosevelt in January 1941 (one of her sisters also performed this mission – see page 28). In May that year she took part in the hunt for the *Bismarck*, the latter being destroyed by gunfire from the *KGV* and the battleship *Rodney*. *King George V* served in Arctic waters on convoy protection duty and in the Mediterranean, where she was attached to Force H to lend fire support to Allied forces landing on Sicily and at Salerno in 1943.

After a refit in 1944 she sailed to join the British Pacific Fleet. In 1945 she carried out many bombardment missions, some against the Japanese home islands; on one occasion, on 9 July 1945, she put down 267 14in shells on the Hitachi factory near Tokyo. *King George V* was decommissioned in 1949 and broken up in 1958.

SPECIFICATIONS

KING GEORGE V

Type: **Battleship**	Armour (deck): **152.6mm (6in)**
Length: **227m (745ft)**	Armour (turrets): **330.2mm (13in)**
Beam: **31.39m (103ft)**	Guns: **10x14in; 8x5.25in**
Draught: **9.6m (31.5ft)**	AA guns: **32x2pdr; 6x20mm**
Displacement (normal): **36,566tnes (35,990t)**	Aircraft: **Three**
Displacement (full load): **41,646tnes (40,990t)**	Crew: **2000**
Machinery: **Boilers & Steam Turbines**	Launched: **February 1939**
Armour (belt): **406.4mm (16in)**	Speed: **28.5 knots**

NELSON

SPECIFICATIONS

NELSON

Type:
Battleship

Length:
216.4m (710ft)

Beam:
32.3m (106ft)

Draught:
10.79m (35.4ft)

Displacement (normal):
36,576tnes (36,000t)

Displacement (full load):
43,830tnes (43,140t)

Machinery:
Boilers & Geared Turbines

Armour (belt):
355.6mm (14in)

Armour (deck):
152.4mm (6in)

Armour (turrets):
406.4mm (16in)

Guns:
9x16in; 12x6in

AA guns:
6x4.7in; 8x2pdr

Aircraft:
None

Crew:
1314

Launched:
September 1925

Speed:
23 knots

HMS *Nelson* and her sister vessel, *Rodney,* were the first British battleships to be constructed after the end of World War I, *Nelson* being launched on 3 September 1925 and completed in June 1927. Her layout was unusual – all her main guns were m,ounted forward. From 1927 to 1941 she was flagship of the Home Fleet, based at Scapa Flow in the Orkneys.

She became an early war casualty, being damaged by a mine off Loch Ewe on 4 September 1939, the day after the outbreak of war, and she did not return to service until August 1940. In the following year she was transferred to the Mediterranean, where she escorted convoys bound for the besieged island of Malta, and on 27 September 1941 she was torpedoed by an Italian aircraft during one such operation, putting her out of action until August 1942.

On 29 September 1943 the armistice agreement with Italy was signed on board her. During the Normandy landings of June 1944 she formed part of the warship force held in reserve for use if necessary by the Western Task Force, and on 12 July she was torpedoed yet again, this time by the German mtor torpedo boat *S138*. After repair at Philadelphia she deployed to the Eastern Fleet, ending her war in the Indian Ocean. She was finally broken up in 1948.

NEWCASTLE

HMS *Newcastle* was one of a class of eight British cruisers, all launched in 1936-37. The others were *Southampton, Birmingham, Glasgow, Sheffield, Liverpool, Manchester* and *Gloucester*. HMS *Newcastle*, originally laid down as *Minotaur*, was the first to be launched, on 23 January 1936.

In 1939–40 she served with the 18th Cruiser Squadron, being based mostly on the river Tyne near her home town. Later in 1940 she deployed to Gibraltar for service in the Mediterranean, and in November took part in the naval engagement with the Italians off Cape Teulada, Sardinia. In 1941 she was engaged in commerce raiding in the South Atlantic, but her main activity during 1941–42 was escorting Mediterranean convoys, providing both defence against enemy naval vessels and ground-based aircraft. This was a highly dangerous mission, especially on the Malta run.

In 1944 she was transferred to the Indian Ocean for convoy protection duties with the Eastern Fleet, her duties also including the escort of aircraft carriers attacking Japanese targets in Sumatra and elsewhere. She was still serving in the Indian Ocean when the war ended. Of the eight ships in this class, three – *Southampton, Manchester* and *Gloucester* – were lost in action in World War II.

SPECIFICATIONS

NEWCASTLE

Type: **Cruiser**	Armour (deck): **50.8mm (2in)**
Length: **180.13m (591ft)**	Armour (turrets): **25.4mm (1in)**
Beam: **19.5m (64ft)**	Guns: **12x6in; 8x4in**
Draught: **6.09m (20ft)**	AA guns: **8x2pdr; 8x.5in**
Displacement (normal): **9469tnes (9320t)**	Aircraft: **Three**
Displacement (full load): **11,725tnes (11,540t)**	Crew: **750**
Machinery: **Steam Turbines**	Launched: **January 1936**
Armour (belt): **123.95mm (4.88in)**	Speed: **32.5 knots**

QUEEN ELIZABETH

SPECIFICATIONS

QUEEN ELIZABETH

Type: **Dreadnought**	Armour (deck): **63.5mm (2.5in)**
Length: **195.98m (643ft)**	Armour (turrets): **330.2mm (13in)**
Beam: **31.69m (104ft)**	Guns: **8x15in; 4x6in**
Draught: **10.21m (33.5ft)**	AA guns: **2x4in**
Displacement (normal): **29,616tnes (29,150t)**	Aircraft: **None**
Displacement (full load): **33,528tnes (33,000t)**	Crew: **951**
Machinery: **Steam Turbines**	Launched: **October 1913**
Armour (belt): **330.2mm (13in)**	Speed: **25 knots**

The "Queen Elizabeth" class of dreadnoughts, laid down in 1912, also included the *Barham*, *Malaya*, *Valiant* and *Warspite*. A sixth vessel, *Agincourt*, was never built. *Queen Elizabeth* was launched on 16 October 1913 and completed in January 1915. She subsequently served on bombardment duty in the ill-starred Dardanelles campaign before rejoining the Grand Fleet, whose flagship she was from 1916 to 1918. However, her anti-aircarft defence was always inadequate

She served in the Mediterranean between the two world wars, undergoing substantial reconstruction in 1926–27 and again in 1937–40. She was recommissioned in January 1941 and based at Alexandria, where in December 1941 she was severely damaged in a daring attack by three Italian "human torpedo" teams, who placed explosive charges under her and her sister ship, HMS *Valiant*. She was made seaworthy and sent to Norfolk, Virginia, for repair, being recommissioned in June 1943. After a spell with the Home Fleet, she was sent to join the Eastern Fleet in the Indian Ocean, where she took part in several bombardment operations against enemy positions in Burma and Sumatra. She was broken up in 1948. She was fortunate to escape the attention of Japanese maritime aircraft, who would have found her an easy prey.

PRINCE OF WALES

Launched on 3 May 1939, the "King George V"-class battleship *Prince of Wales* was the most modern and powerful warship in the Royal Navy when she was completed in March 1941. In fact, she was not fully fitted out when, in May 1941, she was ordered to sea to hunt the German battleship *Bismarck*, and some civilian workmen were still on board. When she came up with *Bismarck* and the heavy cruiser *Prinz Eugen* in the Denmark Strait on 24 May 1941 she received seven hits, compelling her to break off the action. The battlecruiser HMS *Hood* was sunk in this engagement.

In August 1941 the *Prince of Wales* carried Prime Minister Winston Churchill to a meeting with President Roosevelt in Newfoundland; the Atlantic Charter, in which the two Heads of State agreed to co-operate in the defence of their mutual interests, was signed on board her. In December 1941, together with the battlecruiser *Repulse*, the *Prince of Wales* arrived at Singapore, the battleship flying the flag of Admiral Sir Tom Phillips. On 10 December, while searching for a Japanese invasion force, both ships were sunk by enemy bombs and torpedoes, the *Prince of Wales* losing 327 dead, including Admiral Phillips. The attack was proof of the potency of aircraft attack and the eclipse of the battleship as the capital ship of the fleet.

SPECIFICATIONS

PRINCE OF WALES

Type: **Battleship**	Armour (deck): **152.4mm (6in)**
Length: **227.07m (745ft)**	Armour (turrets): **330.2mm (13in)**
Beam: **31.39m (103ft)**	Guns: **10x14in; 8x5.25in**
Draught: **9.6m (31.5ft)**	AA guns: **32x2pdr; 16x.5in**
Displacement (normal): **35,565tnes (35,990t)**	Aircraft: **Two**
Displacement (full load): **41,646tnes (40,990t)**	Crew: **2000**
Machinery: **Steam Turbines**	Launched: **March 1941**
Armour (belt): **406.4mm (16in)**	Speed: **29 knots**

REPULSE

SPECIFICATIONS

REPULSE

Type:
Battlecruiser

Length:
242m (794.25ft)

Beam:
27.43m (90ft)

Draught:
9.67m (31.75ft)

Displacement (normal):
32,512tnes (32,000t)

Displacement (full load):
38,000tnes (37,400t)

Machinery:
Steam Turbines

Armour (belt):
228.6mm (9in)

Armour (deck):
88.9mm (3.5in)

Armour (turrets):
279.4mm (11in)

Guns:
6x15in; 9x4in

AA guns:
24x2pdr; 16x.5in

Aircraft:
Four

Crew:
1309

Launched:
August 1916

Speed:
32 knots

Launched and completed in 1916, the battlecruiser HMS *Repulse* served with the Grand Fleet for the rest of World War I but her active career was curtailed by a collision with the battlecruiser *Australia* in December 1917, in which she was damaged. She underwent a refit in 1921–22, in which her armour protection was increased and torpedo tubes added, and in 1923–24 she undertook a world cruise. She was rated as a potent maritime vessel at the time.

She again underwent a refit in 1932–36; on this occasion her superstructure was built up, an aircraft hangar and catapult were added, and her anti-aircraft armament was increased. After this she served in the Mediterranean until 1938, when she rejoined the British Home Fleet.

At the outbreak of World War II *Repulse* joined other British ships in the search for German blockade runners, and in April 1940 she saw action in Norwegian waters. In May 1941 she took part in the search for the *Bismarck*, and later in the year, together with the *Prince of Wales*, she deployed to the Far East to strengthen the defences of Singapore. It was a fatal decision, for on 10 December, while sailing to operate against Japanese forces, both ships were sunk off the east coast of Malaya by Japanese air attack.

RODNEY

One of the Royal Navy's most famous "battlewagons", the "Nelson" class battleship HMS *Rodney* was named after Admiral Lord George Rodney, a celebrated 18th-century British naval commander. She was launched on 17 December 1925 and completed in August 1927.

At the outbreak of World War II she was with the Home Fleet, imposing the blockade of Germany's merchant commerce in northern waters, and she was in action off Norway at the start of the German invasion, being damaged in an air attack.

After repairs and a refit at Boston, Massachusetts, she returned to active service in 1941 in time to take part in the hunt for the *Bismarck*, which her heavy guns helped to destroy; she was later deployed to Gibraltar for escort duty with the Malta convoys. She formed part of the support force during the Allied invasion of North Africa in November 1942, and in the following year supported the Allied landings on Sicily and in southern Italy.

During the D-Day landings in Normandy, June 1944, she was held in reserve to support the Eastern Task Force if required. However, such was the Allied supremacy during the whole invasion operation that her services were not required. She subsequently returned to escort duties, this time in the Arctic. *Rodney* was broken up in 1948.

SPECIFICATIONS

RODNEY

Type: **Battleship**	Armour (deck): **152.4mm (6in)**
Length: **216.4m (710ft)**	Armour (turrets): **406.4mm (16in)**
Beam: **32.3m (106ft)**	Guns: **9x16in; 12x6in**
Draught: **10.76m (35.3ft)**	AA guns: **6x4.7in; 8x2pdr**
Displacement (normal): **36,576tnes (36,000t)**	Aircraft: **None**
Displacement (full load): **43,830tnes (43,140t)**	Crew: **1314**
Machinery: **Steam Turbines**	Launched: **December 1925**
Armour (belt): **355.6mm (14in)**	Speed: **23 knots**

ROYAL SOVEREIGN

SPECIFICATIONS

ROYAL SOVEREIGN

Type:
Dreadnought

Length:
191.19m (624ft)

Beam:
26.97m (88.5ft)

Draught:
8.68m (28.5ft)

Displacement (normal):
28,448tnes (28,000t)

Displacement (full load):
31,496tnes (31,000t)

Machinery:
Steam Turbines

Armour (belt):
330.2mm (13in)

Armour (deck):
50.8mm (2in)

Armour (turrets):
330.2mm (13in)

Guns:
8x15in; 12x6in

AA guns:
8x4in; 16x2pdr

Aircraft:
One

Crew:
910

Launched:
April 1915

Speed:
21.5 knots

The "Dreadnought" battleship *Royal Sovereign* was launched on 29 April 1915 and completed in 1916, serving with the Grand Fleet for the duration of World War I. She underwent two refits in the years between the wars, and in 1939–41, in service with the Home Fleet, she was assigned to convoy protection in the Atlantic, also operating in the Mediterranean in 1940. In 1941 she underwent a refit and in 1942, together with four other battleships of World War I vintage, she was assigned to the Eastern Fleet in the Indian Ocean.

On 30 May 1944 she was loaned to the Soviet Union and renamed *Arkhangelsk*. Based in the Arctic, she served as the flagship of Admiral Levchenko and led a powerful escort group whose task was to meet incoming convoys and escort them to the Kola inlet. During this period she saw hard service. On 23 August 1944, for example, while escorting Convoy JW59, she was attacked by the *U711*, whose torpedoes detonated prematurely and thus turned out to be harmless.

In September 1944 the *U315* and *U313* both tried to enter the Kola Inlet to attack her, the attempts being frustrated by net barrages; another attempt in January 1945 by "Biber" midget submarines also failed. *Arkhangelsk* was returned to the Royal Navy in February 1949 and sent to the breaker's yard.

SHEFFIELD

HMS *Sheffield* was a "Southampton"-class cruiser, launched on 23 July 1936 and completed in August 1937. At the outbreak of World War II she was serving in the Home Fleet's 2nd Cruiser Squadron. In April 1940 she acted as a troop transport, carrying men of the 146th Infantry Brigade to Norway, and in August she was sent to Gibraltar to become part of Force H for operations in the Mediterranean. In May 1941 she formed part of the force that was sent out to intercept the *Bismarck*, narrowly avoiding a torpedo attack by British Swordfish aircraft, whose crews mistook her for the massive German battleship!

Reassigned to the Home Fleet, she escorted Arctic convoys to Russia, and in December 1942, she was involved in the Battle of the Barents Sea. This was a notable British victory, during which her gunfire damaged the German heavy cruiser *Admiral Hipper* and sank the destroyer *Friedrich Eckoldt*.

In December 1943, with other Royal Navy cruisers, she engaged the German battlecruiser *Scharnhorst* off North Cape, beginning the action that ended with the *Scharnhorst*'s destruction. She later escorted aircraft carriers carrying out strikes against the *Tirpitz*. *Sheffield* was actively involved in the postwar fleet, and was broken up in 1967.

SPECIFICATIONS

SHEFFIELD

Type: **Cruiser**	*Armour (deck):* **38.1mm (1.5in)**
Length: **180.29m (591.5ft)**	*Armour (turrets):* **25.4mm (1in)**
Beam: **18.82m (61.75ft)**	*Guns:* **12x6in; 8x4in**
Draught: **5.18m (17ft)**	*AA guns:* **8x2pdr; 8x.5in**
Displacement (normal): **9246tnes (9100t)**	*Aircraft:* **Two**
Displacement (full load): **11,532tnes (11,350t)**	*Crew:* **750**
Machinery: **Steam Turbines**	*Launched:* **August 1937**
Armour (belt): **114.3mm (4.5in)**	*Speed:* **32 knots**

TRINIDAD

SPECIFICATIONS

TRINIDAD

Type: **Light Cruiser**	Armour (deck): **50.8mm (2in)**
Length: **169.16m (555ft)**	Armour (turrets): **50.8mm (2in)**
Beam: **18.9m (62ft)**	Guns: **12x6in; 8x4in**
Draught: **5.79m (19ft)**	AA guns: **8x2pdr**
Displacement (normal): **9042tnes (8900t)**	Aircraft: **Two**
Displacement (full load): **10,897tnes (10,725t)**	Crew: **730**
Machinery: **Steam Turbines**	Launched: **March 1940**
Armour (belt): **88.9mm (3.5in)**	Speed: **32 knots**

HMS *Trinidad* was one of 11 "Fiji"-class cruisers, and was launched on 21 March 1940, six months after the outbreak of World War II. Her career with the navy was to be interesting.

On 29 March, 1942, while running ahead of an Arctic convoy, she encountered three German destroyers. In a confused engagement in a snowstorm she disabled the destroyer *Z26*, which later sank, but was hit by one of her own torpedoes, which went out of control after being fired to finish off the *Z26*. The submarine *U585* then tried to attack the crippled cruiser, but was sunk by the destroyer *Fury*. The *Trinidad* managed to reach the port of Murmansk, where emergency repairs were made, and on 13 May she set out in company with four destroyers for a point west of Bear Island, where she was to make rendezvous with other British warships. The Russians had promised to provide long-range fighter cover, but only a few aircraft arrived. On the following day *Trinidad* and her escorts were located by enemy air reconnaissance and subjected to torpedo and dive-bomber attacks. One of the latter, delivered by a Junkers Ju 88, hit the *Trinidad* amidships and set her on fire. Bellwoing smoke and badly damaged, the order was given to abandon ship, and *Trinidad* was sunk by the destroyer HMS *Matchless*.

VANGUARD

HMS *Vanguard,* launched on 30 November 1944, was Britain's last battleship and was basically an enlarged "King George V" type, featuring a longer hull to accommodate four twin turrets. Although at this time it was already apparent that she would not be completed before the end of the European war (in fact, she was not completed until April 1946) it was decided to finish her for service in the Pacific, should the war against Japan drag on. Some short cuts were made in her construction, including the installation of the twin 380mm (15in) guns removed from the *Courageous* and *Glorious* when these vessels were converted to aircraft carriers, but many modifications were made as building work progressed and there were inevitable delays.

When she was eventually commissioned she carried the heaviest anti-aircraft armament of any British warship – 71 40mm guns (the lessons that had been learned the hard way by the Royal Navy regarding aerial threats were integrated into this vessel). In 1947 she made headlines when she carried members of the British Royal Family on a state visit to South Africa, and after a refit she served in the Mediterranean in 1949–51, in the training role. After undergoing refits in 1951 and 1954 she was allocated to the reserve in 1956, and was finally broken up in 1960.

SPECIFICATIONS

VANGUARD

Type: **Battleship**	Armour (deck): **152.4mm (6in)**
Length: **243.84m (800ft)**	Armour (turrets): **381mm (15mm)**
Beam: **32.91m (108ft)**	Guns: **8x15in; 16x5.25in**
Draught: **9.22m (30.25ft)**	AA guns: **71x40mm**
Displacement (normal): **45,212tnes (44,500t)**	Aircraft: **None**
Displacement (full load): **52,243tnes (51,420t)**	Crew: **2000**
Machinery: **Steam Turbines**	Launched: **November 1944**
Armour (belt): **406.4mm (16in)**	Speed: **29.5 knots**

VICTORIOUS

SPECIFICATIONS

VICTORIOUS

Type: **Fleet Carrier**	Armour (deck): **76.2mm (3in)**
Length: **243.84m (800ft)**	Armour (turrets): **N/A**
Beam: **28.88 (94.75ft)**	Guns: **None**
Draught: **8.3m (27.75ft)**	AA guns: **8x4.5in; 16x2pdr**
Displacement (normal): **22,709tnes (22,352t)**	Aircraft: **50**
Displacement (full load): **28,593tnes (28,143t)**	Crew: **900**
Machinery: **Steam Turbines**	Launched: **September 1939**
Armour (belt): **101.6mm (4in)**	Speed: **31 knots**

A Fleet Carrier of the "Illustrious" class, HMS *Victorious* saw action in every theatre of World War II. She and her sisters differed from previous carriers in having an armoured hangar, which reduced the number of aircraft that could be carried but greatly increased the vessels' damage resistance level.

Launched on 14 September 1939 and completed in May 1941, *Victorious* was involved in the hunt for the *Bismarck* only days later. In August 1941 she played a key part in Operation Pedestal, a desperate attempt to run supplies through to Malta, and on several occasions she flew off replacement fighters to the island. In 1942–3 she was assigned to convoy protection duty in the Arctic, and in the following year her air group made a series of attacks on the *Tirpitz*.

In 1944 she deployed to the Indian Ocean, her aircraft attacking Japanese oil refineries at Palembang and Sabang, and in January 1945 she sailed for the Pacific, where she saw considerable action off Okinawa during the desperate Japanese defence of the island. She saw considerable service in the postwar years, being completely reconstructed in 1950–57. In November 1967 she was badly damaged by fire at Portsmouth while refitting, and the decision was finally taken to break her up in 1969.

WARSPITE

A Dreadnought of the "Queen Elizabeth" class, HMS *Warspite* probably saw more action than any other modern British warship and was one of the most important Royal Navy vessels of the war. Launched on 26 November 1913 and completed in March 1915, she fought in the Battle of Jutland in the following year, being severely damaged by 14 hits. *Warspite* was substantially reconstructed between the wars and was in action off Norway in April 1940.

Later in the year she bombarded shore targets in the Mediterranean. In March 1941, during the Battle of Cape Matapan, she and HMS *Valiant* destroyed the Italian cruisers *Zara* and *Fiume*, but in May *Warspite* was severely damaged by enemy aircraft off Crete. Returning to service in 1943, she formed part of the naval forces covering the Allied landings on Sicily and at Salerno, being severely damaged by German air-launched glider bombs during the latter operation. It was decided to effect only partial repairs on her, enabling her to be used in the Allied bombardment force covering the D-Day landings in 1944.

Her active career ended when she was damaged by a mine off Harwich on 13 June. On 23 April 1947, while en route to the breaker's yard, she went aground in Mounts Bay, Cornwall, and was broken up in situ.

SPECIFICATIONS

WARSPITE

Type: **Battleship**	Armour (deck): **76.2mm (3in)**
Length: **196.74m (645.5ft)**	Armour (turrets): **330.2mm (13in)**
Beam: **31.7m (104ft)**	Guns: **8x15in; 12x6in**
Draught: **10.05m (33ft)**	AA guns: **8x4.5in; 32x2pdr**
Displacement (normal): **31,816tnes (31,315t)**	Aircraft: **Three**
Displacement (full load): **37,037tnes (36450t)**	Crew: **1200**
Machinery: **Steam Turbines**	Launched: **November 1913**
Armour (belt): **330.2mm (13in)**	Speed: **25 knots**

BANDE NERE

SPECIFICATIONS

BANDE NERE

Type:
Light Cruiser

Length:
169m (554.46ft)

Beam:
15.5m (50.85ft)

Draught:
5.3m (17.38ft)

Displacement (normal):
5283tnes (5200t)

Displacement (full load):
7065tnes (6954t)

Machinery:
Turbines

Armour (belt):
20mm (.78in)

Armour (deck):
24mm (.95in)

Armour (turrets):
23mm (.9in)

Guns:
8x152mm; 6x100mm

AA guns:
3x37mm; 8x13.2mm

Aircraft:
None

Crew:
507

Launched:
October 1928

Speed:
37 knots

The *Bande Nere* – or *Giovanni Delle Bande Nere*, to give the ship her full name – was one of four "Guissano" class light cruisers, laid down for the Italian Navy in 1928. All were destined to be sunk in World War II. They were designed to counter large French destroyers of the "Jaguar", "Lion" and "Aigle" classes.

Bande Nere was launched on 31 October 1928 and completed in April the following year. On 19 July 1940, she and a sister ship, the *Bartolomeo Colleoni*, were engaged by the Australian cruiser *Sydney* and five destroyers in what became known as the Battle of Cape Spada; the *Colleoni* was sunk, 525 of her crew being rescued by the British destroyers, and *Bande Nere* got away after registering a hit on HMAS *Sydney*.

During subsequent operations *Bande Nere* was assigned to the 4th Division, which acted directly under the orders of the Italian Admiralty. Most of the 4th Division's activities involved convoy escort, although it did operate offensively against British Mediterranean convoys. It also undertook some minelaying, mainly in the Sicilian Channel. *Bande Nere* met her end on 1 April 1942, being torpedoed and sunk by the British submarine *Urge* off Stromboli. Though these vessels were fast, they were relatively lightly armed and their anti-aircraft defence was poor.

FIUME

Launched on 27 April 1930 and completed in November 1931, *Fiume* was one of four "Zara"– class heavy cruisers. All four were assigned to the Italian Navy's 1st Division at the time of Italy's entry into the war in June 1940.

In March 1941, with her sister cruisers *Zara* and *Pola* and four destroyers, *Fiume* sailed from Taranto to join other Italian warships in an attempt to intercept British convoys heading for Greece. Much was expected by the Italian High Command, but in the event they were to be very disappointed. The Italian and British Fleets made contact on 28 March, and in the ensuing battle, off Cape Matapan, the battleship *Vittorio Veneto* and the cruiser *Pola* were hit by torpedoes in an air attack by aircraft from the carrier HMS *Formidable*.

The cruisers *Fiume* and *Zara* and the four destroyers were detached to escort the badly damaged *Pola*, while the rest of the Italian warships accompanied the *Vittorio Veneto* to safety. That evening, *Fiume*, *Zara* and *Pole* were detected by radar equipment on the cruiser HMS *Ajax* and a few minutes later were engaged by the battleships *Warspite* and *Valiant*. They were quickly reduced to blazing hulks, being finished off by torpedoes. The crippled *Pola* was also sunk before morning, together with two of her escorting destroyers.

SPECIFICATIONS

FIUME

Type: **Heavy Cruiser**	*Armour (deck):* **70mm (2.75in)**
Length: **182.8m (600ft)**	*Armour (turrets):* **150mm (5.9in)**
Beam: **20.6m (67.58ft)**	*Guns:* **8x203mm; 16x100mm**
Draught: **7.2m (23.62ft)**	*AA guns:* **4x40mm; 8x12.7mm**
Displacement (normal): **11,685tnes (11,500t)**	*Aircraft:* **None**
Displacement (full load): **14,762tnes (14,530t)**	*Crew:* **841**
Machinery: **Eight Boilers**	*Launched:* **April 1930**
Armour (belt): **70mm (2.75in)**	*Speed:* **27 knots**

GORIZIA

SPECIFICATIONS

GORIZIA

Type: **Heavy Cruiser**	Armour (deck): **70mm (2.75in)**
Length: **182.8m (600ft)**	Armour (turrets): **150m (5.9in)**
Beam: **20.6m (67.58ft)**	Guns: **8x203mm; 16x100mm**
Draught: **7.2m (23.62ft)**	AA guns: **4x40mm; 8x12.7mm**
Displacement (normal): **11,685tnes (11,500t)**	Aircraft: **None**
Displacement (full load): **14,762tnes (14,530t)**	Crew: **841**
Machinery: **Eight Boilers**	Launched: **December 1930**
Armour (belt): **70mm (2.75in)**	Speed: **27 knots**

A sister ship of *Fiume*, *Gorizia* was launched on 28 December 1930 and completed exactly a year later. Unlike her three sisters, which were all destroyed, her operational career lasted until Italy's armistice in September 1943 (when Italy switched sides and joined the Allies). From the outset she was involved in attacks on British convoys, albeit without much success, and after the Battle of Cape Matapan, when the Italian Navy was reorganized, she formed part of the 3rd Division with the heavy cruisers *Trento* and *Trieste*. The principal task of the 3rd Division was convoy protection. She took part in the Second Battle of Sirte, and in June 1942 participated in one of the biggest battles of the Mediterranean war, when German and Italian forces combined to launch a costly attack on two convoys bound for Malta.

On 10 April 1943 she was severely damaged in an attack on Maddalena by B-24 bombers of the US Army Air Force (USAAF), and took no further part in the war. On 8 September 1943, following Italy's armistice with the Allies, *Gorizia* was scuttled at La Maddalena. Raised and refloated by the Germans, she was towed to La Spezia, where she was finally sunk on 26 June 1944 by human torpedoes manned by both British and co-belligerent Italian crews.

LANCIERE

The Italian destroyer *Lanciere* was one of the "Soldati" class, all of which were named after types of soldier (*Lancer, Carabinier, Fusilier* and so on). She was launched on 18 December 1938 and completed on 25 March 1939.

From the start of Italy's war in the Mediterranean she was active in defensive minelaying operations off the Italian coast, serving with the 12th Destroyer Division. Like many Italian warships, she woudl see rough handling at the hands of the Royal Navy. During the sea battle off Cape Teulada (Sardinia) in November 1940, for example, she was badly hit by the cruiser HMS *Berwick* and had to be taken in tow, but she was repaired and in action again early in 1941, escorting Axis convoys to Tripoli in North Africa. This was a dangerous duty, and many merchant vessels were sunk by Allied warships and aircraft.

In September 1941, accompanied by other destroyers of her class, she was once again on minelaying duties, sowing minefields to the southeast of Malta. Her eventual fate was strange. In March 1942 she was one of four destroyers that set out from Messina to escort the cruisers *Bande Nere, Gorizia* and *Trento* en route to the Second Battle of Sirte; in the course of that action on 23 March a severe storm blew up, sinking *Lanciere* and another destroyer, *Scirocco*.

SPECIFICATIONS

LANCIERE

Type:
Destroyer

Length:
106m (347.76ft)

Beam:
10.2m (33.46ft)

Draught:
4.35m (14.27ft)

Displacement (normal):
1859tnes (1830t)

Displacement (full load):
2500tnes (2460t)

Machinery:
Turbines

Armour (belt):
Unknown

Armour (deck):
Unknown

Armour (turrets):
Unknown

Guns:
5x120mm

AA guns:
10x20mm

Aircraft:
None

Crew:
187

Launched:
December 1938

Speed:
39 knots

POLA

SPECIFICATIONS

POLA

Type:
Heavy Cruiser

Length:
182.8m (600ft)

Beam:
20.6m (67.58ft)

Draught:
7.2m (23.62ft)

Displacement (normal):
11,685tnes (11,500t)

Displacement (full load):
14,762tnes (14,530t)

Machinery:
Boilers

Armour (belt):
70mm (2.75in)

Armour (deck):
70mm (2.75in)

Armour (turrets):
150mm (5.9in)

Guns:
8x203mm; 16x100mm

AA guns:
4x40mm; 8x12.7mm

Aircraft:
None

Crew:
841

Launched:
December 1931

Speed:
27 knots

The "Zara"-class heavy cruiser *Pola* was launched on 5 December 1931 and completed on 21 December the following year. On Italy's entry into World War II she was assigned to the 3rd Cruiser Division at Messina, together with the *Trento* and *Bolzano*.

In the early naval actions in the Mediterranean, when the Italians had at least some parity with the Royal Navy, she was the flagship of Admiral Paladini. Later in 1940 she was assigned to the 1st Division, and in October she was involved in attempts to intercept heavy units of the Royal Navy heading for Malta with troop reinforcements.

During the battle of Cape Teulada in November 1940 she managed to out-manoeuvre determined attacks by torpedo aircraft from the *Ark Royal*. On 14 December she was damaged in a British air attack on Naples, but repairs were effected in time to sail to take part in the Battle of Cape Matapan. It was to prove a disaster for the Italian Navy, for unknown to its High Command the British were aware of the Italian Fleet's movements through "Ultra" intelligence intercepts. In the night of 28-29 1941 March *Pola* was hit by a torpedo in the course of an air attack and disabled. Further damaged by British gunfire, she was fatally damaged and thus abandoned by her crew. Her hull was finished off by several British destroyers.

VITTORIO VENETO

The Italian battleship *Vittorio Veneto*, whose name commemorated the Italian Army's victory over the Austrians on 3 November 1918, was launched on 22 July 1937 and completed in April 1940. She was one of th emost powerful vessels in the Italians Navy, and much was expected of her.

She narrowly missed being damaged in the Fleet Air Arm torpedo attack on Taranto in November 1940, and again when she put to sea later in the month. In the Battle of Cape Matapan, March 1941, she was attacked by torpedo-carrying Swordfish aircraft from the carrier HMS *Formidable*. Three torpedoes were dropped at close range and one of them struck her just above her port outer propeller, quickly flooding her with thousands of tons of water.

The Italian commander, Admiral Iachino (the *Veneto* was his flagship), broke off the action and units of his fleet escorted the battleship to safety. On 14 December 1941 she was torpedoed by the British submarine *Urge* while escorting a convoy to Libya, and in June she was further damaged in a US air attack on *La Spezia*. The *Veneto* surrendered to the Allies in September 1943 and was interned in the Suez Canal until 1946. It took several years to strip her down, and she was finally broken up at La Spezia in 1960.

SPECIFICATIONS

VITTORIO VENETO

Type:
Battleship

Length:
237.8m (780ft)

Beam:
32.9m (107.93ft)

Draught:
10.5m (34.49ft)

Displacement (normal):
41,167tnes (40,517t)

Displacement (full load):
46,484tnes (45,752t)

Machinery:
Boilers

Armour (belt):
350mm (13.79in)

Armour (deck):
10mm (.39in)

Armour (turrets):
350mm (13.79in)

Guns:
9x12in; 12x6in; 12x90mm

AA guns:
20x37mm

Aircraft:
Three

Crew:
1920

Launched:
July 1937

Speed:
30 knots

ZARA

SPECIFICATIONS

ZARA

Type: **Heavy Cruiser**	Armour (deck): **70mm (2.75in)**
Length: **182.8m (600ft)**	Armour (turrets): **150mm (5.9in)**
Beam: **20.6m (67.58ft)**	Guns: **8x203mm; 16x100mm**
Draught: **7.2m (23.62ft)**	AA guns: **4x40mm; 8x12.7mm**
Displacement (normal): **11,685tnes (11,500t)**	Aircraft: **None**
Displacement (full load): **14,762tnes (14,530t)**	Crew: **841**
Machinery: **Boilers**	Launched: **April 1930**
Armour (belt): **70mm (2.75in)**	Speed: **33 knots**

*Z*ara was class leader of a group of four heavy cruisers, the others being *Fiume, Gorizia* and *Pola*. She was launched on 27 April 1930, completed on 20 October 1931, and her operational career almost exactly matched that of her sister ships *Fiume* and *Pola*, all three vessels being sunk by the British at the Battle of Cape Matapan in March 1941.

The "Zara" class ships, originally classed at light cruisers, then armoured cruisers and finally heavy cruisers, were intended to be an improvement on the earlier "Trento" class, completed in the 1920s. However, the experiment was not a success. It was soon realised that the intended increase in armour protection, speed and gunnery could not be provided under the 10,160-tonne (10,000-ton) limit imposed by the various naval treaties between the wars, although when completed the displacement of the vessels exceeded the treaty limit by 1524 tonnes (1500 tons).

All four ships were equipped with a launch catapult and a hangar capable of accommodating two spotter aircraft was fitted beneath the forecastle. Although the ships were capable of over 33 knots, higher speed was sacrificed for greater armour protection; in fact, the weight of armour installed was three times that of the "Trento" class.

AKAGI

Akagi, named after a mountain northwest of Tokyo, was originally laid down as a high-speed battlecruiser, one of a class of four. The other three (*Amagi, Atago* and *Takao*) were cancelled in 1922 because of the restrictions imposed by the Washington Naval Treaty and construction of *Akagi* was suspended when she was 40 per cent complete, but in 1923 it was decided to re-order *Akagi* as an aircraft carrier. The decision was a good one with regard to the type of war the navy would fight in the Pacific Ocean.

She was launched in her new guise on 22 April 1925 and completed in March 1927. In her original aircraft carrier configuration she had three flight decks forward, no island and two funnels on the starboard side, but during substantial reconstruction in 1935–38 the two lower flight decks forward were removed and the top flight deck extended forward to the bow. An island was also added on the port side.

In December 1941 *Akagi* was part of the carrier task force that attacked Pearl Harbor; in subsequent operations her aircraft also attacked targets on Rabaul, Java and Ceylon and took part in raids on Darwin early in 1942. On 4 June 1942 *Akagi* was severely damaged by US aircraft at the Battle of Midway and had to be sunk by the destroyers *Nowake* and *Arashi*.

SPECIFICATIONS

AKAGI

Type: Aircraft Carrier	**Armour (deck):** 76.2mm (3in)
Length: 261m (856ft)	**Armour (turrets):** N/A
Beam: 31.4m (103ft)	**Guns:** 6x102mm; 12x127mm
Draught: 8.7m (28.54ft)	**AA guns:** 28x25mm
Displacement (normal): 37,084tnes (36,500t)	**Aircraft:** 91
Displacement (full load): 41,961tnes (41,300t)	**Crew:** 2000
Machinery: Steam Turbines	**Launched:** April 1925
Armour (belt): 152.4mm (6in)	**Speed:** 31.5 knots

HARUNA

SPECIFICATIONS

HARUNA

Type:
Battlecruiser

Length:
215m (704ft)

Beam:
28.04m (92ft)

Draught:
8.38m (27.5ft)

Displacement (normal):
27,940tnes (27,500t)

Displacement (full load):
32,817tnes (32,300t)

Machinery:
Steam Turbines

Armour (belt):
203.2mm (8in)

Armour (deck):
55.88mm (2.2in)

Armour (turrets):
228.6mm (9in)

Guns:
8x14in; 16x6in; 8x3in

AA guns:
None

Aircraft:
Three

Crew:
1221

Launched:
December 1913

Speed:
27 knots

The battlecruiser *Haruna* and her three sisters, *Hiei*, *Kirishima* and *Kongo*, were designed by an Englishman, Sir George Thurston, and embodied some improvements based on experience with the British "Lion" class. *Haruna* was launched on 14 December 1913 and completed in April 1915. All four ships underwent two periods of extensive reconstruction between the wars, after which they were reclassified as battleships. A major problem with all the ships was the lack of proper anti-aircraft defences.

In December 1941 she formed part of the naval force covering the Japanese landings in Malaya and the East Indies, and escorted the aircraft carriers whose aircraft carried out a major attack on Darwin in February 1942 and on Ceylon in April.

In June 1942 she took part in the Battle of Midway, and later on she participated in the Battles of Guadalcanal, Santa Cruz, Philippine Sea and Leyte Gulf. During the Battle of the Philippine Sea, she was damaged by air attack on 19 June 1944. On 18 March 1945 she was again damaged by air attack while at anchor off Kure, and on 28 July she was sunk by US carrier aircraft at that same location. She was refloated and broken up at Harima in 1946. The name *Haruna* derives from a mountain in north central Honshu.

HIEI

Asister ship of *Haruna,* the battlecruiser *Hiei* – reclassified as a battleship after reconstruction in the 1930s – was launched on 21 November 1912 and completed on 4 August 1914. A few weeks later she took part in the search for the German Admiral von Spee's South Atlantic Squadron, which was eventually destroyed by the Royal Navy off the Falkland Islands. Between periods of reconstruction *Hiei* – which was demilitarized under the terms of the London Naval Treaty of 1922 – was used as a cadet training ship. During World War II she performed well enough when the Japanese had aerial supremacy, but was very vulnerable when this was not the case.

Fully modernized by 1941, she formed part of the Japanese task force whose carrier aircraft attacked Pearl Harbor, and subsequently saw action during the invasion of the East Indies – when she and the *Kirishima* sank the US destroyer *Edsall* south of Java – the attack on Ceylon, and the Battles of Midway, the Eastern Solomons, Santa Cruz and Guadalcanal. During the latter operation, in what became known as the First Battle of Guadalcanal, she was sunk by American gunfire, torpedoes and air attack off Savo Island on 13 November 1942. This action took place at night, the US warships involved having the major advantage of radar.

SPECIFICATIONS

HIEI

Type: **Battlecruiser**	Armour (deck): **55.88mm (2.2in)**
Length: **214.57m (704ft)**	Armour (turrets): **228.6mm (9in)**
Beam: **28.04m (92ft)**	Guns: **8x14in; 16x6in; 8x3in**
Draught: **8.38m (27.5ft)**	AA guns: **None**
Displacement (normal): **27,940tnes (27,500t)**	Aircraft: **Three**
Displacement (full load): **32,817tnes (32,300t)**	Crew: **1201**
Machinery: **Boilers & Steam Turbines**	Launched: **November 1912**
Armour (belt): **203.2mm (8in)**	Speed: **27 knots**

HOSHO

SPECIFICATIONS

HOSHO

Type:
Aircraft Carrier

Length:
248m (813.64ft)

Beam:
32.6m (107ft)

Draught:
9.5m (31.17ft)

Displacement (normal):
7590tnes (7470t)

Displacement (full load):
9785tnes (9630t)

Machinery:
Steam Turbines

Armour (belt):
None

Armour (deck):
None

Armour (turrets):
N/A

Guns:
4x140mm

AA guns:
8x25mm

Aircraft:
21

Crew:
550

Launched:
November 1921

Speed:
25 knots

Originally projected in 1919 as an auxiliary tanker capable of carrying aircraft, *Hosho*, whose name means "Soaring Phoenix", was in fact completed as Japan's first dedicated aircraft carrier, being launched on 13 November 1921 and completed in December 1922. Built with British assistance, she was extensively used for trials and development work. She had a small bridge and three funnels, which could be swung down during flying operations; the bridge was removed in 1923 and the flight deck made flush to improve aircraft operation. *Hosho* was also fitted with a system of mirrors and lights to assist pilots in landing. It was by such measures and training that the Japanese naval pilots were among the best in the world when war broke out in 1941.

During the Sino-Japanese war *Hosho*'s air group was used to provide close air support; she was afterwards relegated to the training role, but became operational again on Japan's entry into World War II and saw active service during the Battle of Midway before reverting to training duties. On 19 March 1945 she was damaged in an air attack on the naval base at Kure (her antiaircraft defences were totally inadequate at this time), and was disarmed on 20 April. At the war's end she was used to repatriate prisoners of war, and was broken up at Osaka in April 1947.

HYUGA

A Dreadnought of the "Ise" class, *Hyuga,* named after a province of southeast Kyushu, was launched on 27 January 1917 and completed in April 1918. In 1934–36, in common with other capital ships of the Imperial Japanese Navy, she underwent a complete reconstruction, improvements including thicker deck armour and the addition of anti-torpedo bulges.

In June 1942 she formed part of the escort force whose carriers launched their aircraft at the island of Midway. As a result of the staggering carrier losses sustained by the Japanese in this battle, *Hyuga* and others of her class were converted as "battleship-carriers" in 1943, being fitted with a hangar which could house 22 seaplanes. The idea was that all the aircraft would be catapult-launched in 20 minutes, alighting on the sea on their return and being hoisted aboard by cranes. The scheme was not tested in combat because of a critical shortage of both aircraft and pilots (by this stage of the war the Americans had such a superiority in carriers and aircraft that it would have made little difference).

Hyuga was in action during the Battle of Leyte Gulf, where she formed part of a decoy force. She was deactivated on 1 March 1945 and sunk in shallow water near Kure by US aircraft on 24 July. *Hyuga* was refloated and broken up in 1952.

SPECIFICATIONS

HYUGA

Type: **Dreadnought**	Armour (deck): **76.2mm (3in)**
Length: **205.74m (675ft)**	Armour (turrets): **304.8mm (12in)**
Beam: **28.65m (94ft)**	Guns: **12x14in; 20x5.5in; 4x3in**
Draught: **8.83m (29ft)**	AA guns: **None**
Displacement (normal): **31,760tnes (31,260t)**	Aircraft: **None**
Displacement (full load): **37,084tnes (36,500t)**	Crew: **1360**
Machinery: **Boilers & Steam Turbines**	Launched: **January 1917**
Armour (belt): **304.8mm (12in)**	Speed: **23 knots**

KAGA

SPECIFICATIONS

KAGA

Type: **Aircraft Carrier**	Armour (deck): **58.42mm (2.3in)**
Length: **240.48m (789ft)**	Armour (turrets): **N/A**
Beam: **32.91m (108ft)**	Guns: **None**
Draught: **9.44m (31ft)**	AA guns: **25x20mm; 30x13.2mm**
Displacement (normal): **26,417tnes (26,000t)**	Aircraft: **85**
Displacement (full load): **34,233tnes (33,693t)**	Crew: **1340**
Machinery: **Boilers & Steam Turbines**	Launched: **November 1920**
Armour (belt): **279.4mm (11in)**	Speed: **27.5 knots**

*K*aga was laid down as a battleship and launched on 17 November 1920. Under the terms of the 1921 Washington Treaty she was to have been scrapped, but instead the Imperial Japanese Navy decided to complete her as an aircraft carrier to replace another carrier, the *Amagi*, which had been destroyed in an earthquake while under construction. She was completed in March 1928 and joined the Combined Fleet in 1930. In 1934–35 she was reconstructed, a full-length flight deck and island being added. This made her one of the major aircraft carriers in the navy at the beginning of the war in December 1941.

Recommissioned in June 1935, she was assigned to the First Carrier Division with the *Akagi*, her air group seeing action during the Sino-Japanese war. Her career during World War II was short but spectacular.

In December 1941 her aircraft attacked Pearl Harbour, and subsequently operated over Rabaul, Darwin and Java. She then formed part of the Japanese carrier task force assembled for the assault on Midway Island. Concentrating on the destruction of Midway's air defences, the Japanese carriers were caught unprepared when American dive-bombers and torpedo-bombers launched their counter-attack; *Akagi*, *Kaga* and *Soryu* were all sunk, *Kaga* suffering 800 dead.

KIRISHIMA

The "Kongo"-class battlecruiser *Kirishima* (named after a mountain in Kyushu) was launched on 1 December 1913 and completed in April 1915. In the 1930s, like others of her kind, she underwent major reconstruction and was reclassified as a battleship in preparation for the war in the Pacific Ocean. As well as having a formidable main armament, she was well equipped with antiaircraft guns.

In December 1941 she was assigned to escort the carriers whose aircraft attacked Pearl Harbor; she subsequently covered the Japanese landings at Rabaul and in the Dutch East Indies, and on 1 March 1942 she assisted in the sinking of the destroyer USS *Edsall* south of Java. In the months that followed she participated in almost all Japanese naval actions in the South Pacific. During the naval battles near the Santa Cruz islands, preceding the assault on Guadalcanal, she bore an apparently charmed life; on 25 October 1942 she experienced several near misses when Boeing B-17s bombed her and she was attacked by torpedo-armed aircraft. In November she bombarded Henderson Field on Guadalcanal in support of a Japanese invasion force. Her luck finally ran out on 15 November 1942, though, when she was sunk by the gunfire of the US battleship *Washington*.

SPECIFICATIONS

KIRISHIMA

Type: **Battlecruiser**	Armour (deck): **55.88mm (2.2in)**
Length: **214.67m (704ft)**	Armour (turrets): **228.6mm (9in)**
Beam: **28.04m (92ft)**	Guns: **8x14in; 16x6in; 8x3in**
Draught: **8.38m (27.5ft)**	AA guns: **4x40mm; 8x13.2mm**
Displacement (normal): **27,940tnes (27,500t)**	Aircraft: **Three**
Displacement (full load): **32,817tnes (32,300t)**	Crew: **1221**
Machinery: **Boilers & Steam Turbines**	Launched: **December 1913**
Armour (belt): **203.2mm (8in)**	Speed: **27 knots**

KONGO

SPECIFICATIONS

KONGO

Type:
Battlecruiser

Length:
214.57m (704ft)

Beam:
28.04m (92ft)

Draught:
8.38m (27.5ft)

Displacement (normal):
27,940tnes (27,500t)

Displacement (full load):
32,817tnes (32,300t)

Machinery:
Steam Turbines

Armour (belt):
203.2mm (8in)

Armour (deck):
55.88mm (2.2in)

Armour (turrets):
228.6mm (9in)

Guns:
8x14in; 16x6in; 8x3in

AA guns:
4x40mm; 8x13.2mm

Aircraft:
Three

Crew:
1201

Launched:
May 1912

Speed:
27 knots

The battlecruiser *Kongo* was built by the British firm Vickers-Armstrong at Barrow-in-Furness, England, and was the first ship in the Imperial Japanese Navy to be fitted with 355mm (14in) guns (her construction shows the good relationships between the British and the Japanese at this period). She was launched on 18 May 1912 and completed in August 1913. In the early weeks of World War I she took part in the search for Admiral von Spee's South Atlantic Squadron, which destroyed a British naval force at Coronel before being itself destroyed off the Falkland Islands.

Between the two world wars *Kongo* underwent two periods of reconstruction, after which she was reclassed as a high-speed battleship. After the outbreak of the Pacific war she was an active member of the fleet: she covered the Japanese landings in Malaya, formed part of the force escorting the aircraft carriers whose aircraft attacked Darwin and Ceylon, and in June 1942, as part of the 3rd Battleship Squadron, she formed a key escort element of the force that was to have invaded Midway Island. She featured in the battles of Guadalcanal, Santa Cruz, the Philippine Sea and Leyte Gulf, and on 21 November 1944 she was torpedoed and sunk by the submarine USS *Sealion* some 105km (65 miles) northwest of Keelung.

MOGAMI

The four ships of the "Mogami" light cruiser class were designed to mount the heaviest possible armament on the restricted tonnage set by the London Naval Treaty of 1930. They featured triple gun turrets and, following the example of Germany's "pocket battleships", their hulls were electrically welded to save weight. During trials, however, they proved to be unstable, and the first two ships – *Mogami* and *Mikuma* – were taken out of service for alterations.

Launched on 14 March 1934, *Mogami* and *Mikuma* both took part in the Battle of Midway in June 1942, the former being sunk and the latter severely damaged by carrier aircraft from the USS *Yorktown*. After repairs *Mogami* was returned to service in 1943, having been fitted with a flight deck on which it was intended to carry 11 seaplanes (as part of the Japanese's desperate attempt to augment their naval air power following severe losses). The cruiser was again damaged in action off the Solomons in July 1943; repaired a second time, she was back in service with the 7th Cruiser Squadron in 1944. On 25 October she was sunk by air attack at the Battle of the Surigao Strait. None of the other ships of the "Mogami" class survived the war; *Suzuya* was lost at the Battle of Leyte Gulf and *Kumano* was sunk by US aircraft in Colon Bay.

SPECIFICATIONS

MOGAMI

Type: Cruiser	**Armour (deck):** 38mm (1.5in)
Length: 200m (656.16ft)	**Armour (turrets):** 127mm (5in)
Beam: 20.5m (65.61ft)	**Guns:** 15x155mm; 8x127mm
Draught: 10.9m (35.76ft)	**AA guns:** 8x25mm
Displacement (normal): 12,599tnes (12,400t)	**Aircraft:** Three
Displacement (full load): 13,188tnes (12,980t)	**Crew:** 930
Machinery: Geared Turbines	**Launched:** March 1934
Armour (belt): 100mm (3.93in)	**Speed:** 36 knots

MUTSU

SPECIFICATIONS

MUTSU

Type:
Battleship

Length:
213.36m (700ft)

Beam:
28.95m (95ft)

Draught:
9.14m (30ft)

Displacement (normal):
34,431tnes (33,800t)

Displacement (full load):
39,116tnes (38,500t)

Machinery:
Steam Turbines

Armour (belt):
304.8mm (12in)

Armour (deck):
76.2mm (3in)

Armour (turrets):
355.6mm (14in)

Guns:
8x16in; 20x5.5in; 4x3in

AA guns:
20x25mm

Aircraft:
Three

Crew:
1333

Launched:
May 1920

Speed:
25 knots

Launched on 31 May 1920 and completed in October 1921, the "Dreadnought" battleship *Mutsu* (an ancient name for the provinces of northern Honshu) was the second warship of the "Nagato" class. She was extensively modified in two refits between the wars. In 1934–36, based at Yokosuka, she was used for long-range reconnaissance in the Pacific, gathering much information which was of great value when the Imperial Japanese Navy went to war five years later (though the activities of such a large ship seem to have totally eluded the Americans).

In June 1942, at the Battle of Midway, she was part of the Midway Support Group, which came under the direct orders of Admiral Yamamoto and also included the battleships *Nagato* and *Yamato*. In July 1942, following the abortive Midway operation, *Mutsu* was assigned to the 2nd Battleship Squadron of the First Fleet under Vice-Admiral Takasu, together with the battleships *Nagato*, *Fuso* and *Yamashiro*.

In August 1942, during the battle off the Solomon Islands that preceded the Japanese landings on Guadalcanal, she led a support group that included the seaplane carrier *Chitose*. On 8 June 1942, while at anchor in Hiroshima Bay, *Mutsu* was destroyed by an internal magazine explosion with the loss of 1222 lives.

MYOKO

Myoko was the leader of a class of 10,160-tonne (10,000-ton) cruisers, the others being *Ashigara*, *Haguro* and *Nachi*. She was launched on 16 April 1927. As with other cruiser classes of this period, the "Myokos", thanks to advanced design and shipbuilding techniques, mounted the maximum armament and achieved the highest possible speeds while conforming to the tonnage restrictions of the Washington Treaty. They were useful vessels, and would prove their worth during the campaign in the Pacific, though they all suffered at the hands of the Alllies.

During World War II the ships of this class formed the Fifth Cruiser Division. In December 1941 they participated in the Japanese landings in the Philippines, and all their subsequent operations were conducted in the area of the Dutch East Indies, Malaya. and the Philippines. On 24 October 1944, during Allied operations to recapture the Philippines, *Myoko* was torpedoed by an American aircraft and deemed to be a constructive total loss on 13 December.

Of the other ships in the class, *Nachi* was sunk by US air attack in Manila Bay in November 1944; *Haguro* was sunk by British destroyers off Penang in May 1945; and *Ashigara* was sunk in June 1945 in the Bangka Strait, Indonesia, by the British submarine *Trenchant*.

SPECIFICATIONS

MYOKO

Type: Cruiser	**Armour (deck):** 127mm (5in)
Length: 207m (679.13ft)	**Armour (turrets):** 76.2mm (3in)
Beam: 19m (62.33ft)	**Guns:** 10x203mm; 6x120mm
Draught: 6.3m (20.75ft)	**AA guns:** 8x25mm
Displacement (normal): 12,568tnes (12,370t)	**Aircraft:** Two
Displacement (full load): 13,594tnes (13,380t)	**Crew:** 792
Machinery: Geared Turbines	**Launched:** April 1927
Armour (belt): 102mm (4.01in)	**Speed:** 33 knots

NAGATO

SPECIFICATIONS

NAGATO

Type:
Battleship

Length:
213.36m (700ft)

Beam:
28.95m (95ft)

Draught:
9.14m (30ft)

Displacement (normal):
34,341tnes (33,800t)

Displacement (full load):
39,116tnes (38,500t)

Machinery:
Steam Turbines

Armour (belt):
304.8mm (12in)

Armour (deck):
76.2mm (3in)

Armour (turrets):
355.6mm (14in)

Guns:
8x16in; 20x5.5in

AA guns:
20x25mm

Aircraft:
Three

Crew:
1333

Launched:
November 1919

Speed:
27 knots

The two ships of the "Nagato" class (the other was the *Mutsu*) were laid down in the closing stages of World War one as part of the Japanese Navy's so-called "8-8" programme, which envisaged the building of eight battleships and eight battlecruisers. Launched on 9 November 1919, *Nagato* was completed in November 1920.

During substantial reconstruction work at Kure in 1934–36, her fore funnel was removed, she was re-engined and re-boilered, anti-torpedo bulges were added, the elevation of her main armament was increased to give the guns a better anti-aircraft capability (though using main guns to shoot down aircraft appears to have been a desperate measure), and a clipper bow was fitted. During the early months of the Pacific War she was flagship of the Imperial Japanese Combined Fleet, and as such she saw action at Midway and in the Battle of the Philippine Sea.

In October 1944, during the Battle of Leyte Gulf, she was damaged by aircraft bombs at Samar. She took no further part in the war, being laid up at Yokosuka, and surrendered to the Allies there in September 1945. In July 1946 she was used as a target ship for the US nuclear tests at Bikini; severely damaged in the second test, she sank on 29 July.

SHIMAKAZE

Laid down on 8 August 1941, *Shimakaze* was essentially an experimental destroyer, being fitted with engines of a new design that worked at an exceptionally high temperature and pressure, giving the ship a top speed of just under 40 knots. However, her good speed was negated somewhat by the role she was to undertake during the war.

Launched on 18 July 1942, *Shimakaze* took part in the evacuation of Japanese forces from the island of Kiska, in the Aleutians, in August 1943. October that year saw her operating in the South Pacific, covering a carrier task force operating in the area of the Solomons, and in May 1944 she was part of the Japanese naval forces tasked with the defence of the Marianas island chain. *Shimakaze*'s role remained primarily that of escorting carrier groups, which she undertook in the Battle of the Philippine Sea in June 1944.

She subsequently escorted Japanese troop convoys, and it was in this role that she met her end. On 11 November 1944, with other destroyers, she was escorting a large troop convoy attempting to land reinforcements at Ormoc, Leyte, when the naval force was subjected to heavy air attack. Four destroyers, *Shimakaze* included, were sunk, as were five transports. Only a fraction of the Japanese troops on the latter reached the shore.

SPECIFICATIONS

SHIMAKAZE

Type: **Destroyer**	Armour (deck): **Unknown**
Length: **99.5m (326.44ft)**	Armour (turrets): **Unknown**
Beam: **Unknown**	Guns: **4x120mm**
Draught: **Unknown**	AA guns: **2x7.7mm**
Displacement (normal): **1388tnes (1366t)**	Aircraft: **None**
Displacement (full load): **1703tnes (1676t)**	Crew: **148**
Machinery: **Geared Turbines**	Launched: **July 1942**
Armour (belt): **Unknown**	Speed: **39 knots**

TAKAO

SPECIFICATIONS

TAKAO

Type:
Cruiser

Length:
204.7m (671.58ft)

Beam:
19m (62.33ft)

Draught:
10.9m (35.76ft)

Displacement (normal):
41,878tnes (41,217t)

Displacement (full load):
47,754tnes (47,000t)

Machinery:
Geared Turbines

Armour (belt):
102mm (4.01in)

Armour (deck):
76.2mm (3in)

Armour (turrets):
76.2mm (3in)

Guns:
10x203mm; 4x120mm

AA guns:
2x40mm

Aircraft:
Three

Crew:
762

Launched:
May 1930

Speed:
35 knots

Launched on 12 May 1930, the heavy cruiser *Takao* was leader of a class of four, the others being *Chokai*, *Atago* and *Maya*. *Takao* was refitted and modernized in 1939–40. As part of the 4th Cruiser Squadron, she covered the Japanese landings in Malaya and on Luzon in December 1941, and also the landings in the Dutch East Indies in January 1942.

In June 1942, she formed part of the Japanese carrier force at the Battle of Midway, which saw the turn of the tide in the Pacific war. August 1942 saw her operating in the Solomons area, and in the battle for Guadalcanal her gunfire inflicted heavy damage on the US battleship *South Dakota*. In November 1943 she was severely damaged by US air attack while covering the movement of Japanese forces in the Truk/Rabaul area; on returning to active duty she formed part of the defence of the Marianas.

In June 1944 she participated in the Battle of the Philippine Sea. In October 1944, during the battle for Leyte, she was torpedoed by the US submarine *Darter*. Transferred to the Indian Ocean after repair, on 30 July 1945 she was attacked in Singapore harbour by British midget submarines and was so badly damaged by their charges that she sank. Refloated after the war, she was scuttled in the Malacca Straits in 1946.

YAMATO

The *Yamato* and her sister ship, *Musashi*, whose construction was carried out in great secrecy, were the largest and most powerful battleships ever built, and were designed to outfight – or at least compete on equal terms with – any group of enemy battleships. Four ships were planned, but the third, *Shinano*, was completed as an aircraft carrier, and the fourth was never launched.

Yamato was launched on 8 August 1940 and completed in December 1941. It was ironic that she should be obsolete even before she was launched – the day of the battleship was over. As flagship of the Combined Fleet she saw action in the battles of Midway and the Philippine Sea, being damaged by bombs from US aircraft. She received further damage on 25 December 1943, when she was torpedoed by the submarine USS *Skate* off Truk.

Yamato and *Musashi* both took part in the great air and sea battles at Leyte Gulf, *Musashi* sinking on 24 October 1944 after receiving numerous bomb and torpedo hits. *Yamato* herself was also damaged in this battle by two American bombs. On 7 April 1945 *Yamato* sailed from Japan on what was virtually a suicide mission against the Allied naval forces assembled off Okinawa, and was sunk by US carrier aircraft 210km (130 miles) southwest of Kagoshima with the loss of 2498 lives.

SPECIFICATIONS

YAMATO

Type:
Battleship

Length:
262.89m (862.5ft)

Beam:
36.88m (121ft)

Draught:
10.36m (34ft)

Displacement (normal):
64,008tnes (63,000t)

Displacement (full load):
72,806tnes (71,659t)

Machinery:
Steam Turbines

Armour (belt):
409mm (16.1in)

Armour (deck):
198.12mm (7.8in)

Armour (turrets):
635mm (25in)

Guns:
19x18in; 12x6in; 12x5in

AA guns:
24x25mm; 1x13.2mm

Aircraft:
Five

Crew:
2500

Launched:
August 1940

Speed:
27 knots

ZUIHO

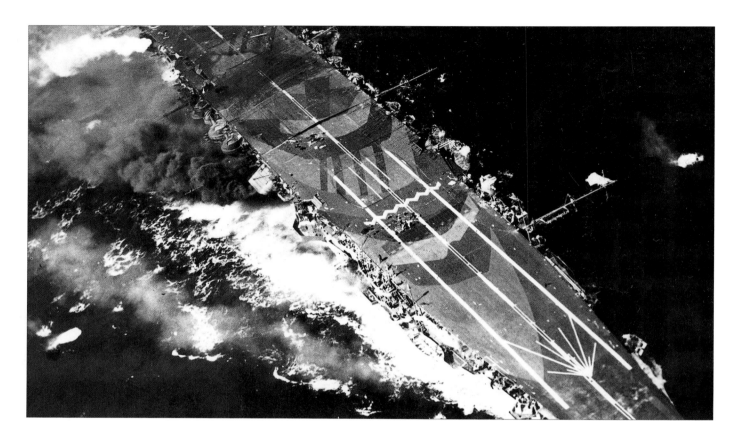

SPECIFICATIONS

ZUIHO

Type: **Aircraft Carrier**	**Armour (deck):** **None**
Length: **217m (712ft)**	**Armour (turrets):** **N/A**
Beam: **18m (59.05ft)**	**Guns:** **8x127mm**
Draught: **6.6m (21.65ft)**	**AA guns:** **15x25mm**
Displacement (normal): **11,446tnes (11,266t)**	**Aircraft:** **30**
Displacement (full load): **14,427tnes (14,200t)**	**Crew:** **785**
Machinery: **Steam Turbines**	**Launched:** **June 1936**
Armour (belt): **None**	**Speed:** **28 knots**

The light carrier *Zuiho* was originally laid down in 1935 at Yokosuka as the submarine depot ship *Takasaki*. Launched on 19 June 1936, she was re-ordered as an aircraft carrier in 1940 and renamed *Zuiho* ("Lucky Phoenix"), being completed in December that year. Her aircraft complement was not large, but she provided valuable service during the battles in the Pacific Ocean with the Americans. From the beginning, though, her anti-aircraft armament was too light.

In June 1942 her air group was to have provided close support for the Japanese invasion force in the Battle of Midway, and in September she sailed from Truk as part of the naval forces designated to support operations on Guadalcanal. However, on 26 October 1942 she was damaged by aircraft bombs at the Battle of Santa Cruz.

In April 1943 she provided reinforcements for the 11th Air Fleet on Rabaul and Buka in preparation for the last Japanese air offensive in the Solomons; further reinforcements were flown in during October. In October 1944, at Leyte, she formed part of a diversionary force under Admiral Ozawa, its task to draw the American Task Force 58 away from the main Japanese striking force. In the ensuing action, on 25 October 1944, she was sunk by US carrier aircraft northeast of Cape Engano, along with three other carriers.

ZUIKAKU

The Fleet Carriers *Zuikaku* ("Lucky Crane") and *Shokaku* ("Happy Crane") were both laid down after the expiry of the Naval Treaties of the 1930s, and consequently no limitations were placed on their design. They had strengthened flight decks, a very long range, and were capable of 34 knots. However, armament against aerial attack was rather neglected, which would prove fata.

The vessels formed part the 5th Carrier Squadron of Admiral Nagumo's 1st Naval Air Fleet, and took part in the attack on Pearl Harbor on 7 December 1941. *Zuikaku* subsequently took part in every Japanese naval action of the Pacific war up to and including the Battle of Leyte Gulf, with the exception of the Battle of Midway; her absence, and that of *Shokaku*, was due to a shortage of maritime aviation pilots and to substantial damage sustained in the Battle of the Coral Sea, where *Shokaku* received three bombs hits. *Shokaku* was sunk by three torpedoes from the US submarine *Cavalla* on 19 June 1944, during the Battle of the Philippine Sea; *Zuikaku* survived a little longer to take part in the Battle of Leyte Gulf, but on 25 October 1944 she was sunk in a massive attack by 326 American dive-bombers and torpedo aircraft, which also destroyed the carriers *Chitose*, *Zuiho* and *Chiyoda*.

SPECIFICATIONS

ZUIKAKU

Type: **Aircraft Carrier**	Armour (deck): **129.54mm (5.1in)**
Length: **257.5m (844.81ft)**	Armour (turrets): **N/A**
Beam: **28m (91.86ft)**	Guns: **16x127mm**
Draught: **8.9m (29.19ft)**	AA guns: **36x25mm**
Displacement (normal): **26,086tnes (25,675t)**	Aircraft: **84**
Displacement (full load): **32,618tnes (32,105t)**	Crew: **1660**
Machinery: **Steam Turbines**	Launched: **November 1939**
Armour (belt): **165.1mm (6.5in)**	Speed: **34.2 knots**

ALABAMA

SPECIFICATIONS

ALABAMA

Type: **Battleship**	Armour (deck): **38.1mm (1.5in)**
Length: **207.26m (680ft)**	Armour (turrets): **457.2mm (18in)**
Beam: **32.91m (108ft)**	Guns: **9x16in; 36x5in**
Draught: **8.91m (29.25ft)**	AA guns: **28x1.1in; 24x40mm**
Displacement (normal): **35,966tnes (35,400t)**	Aircraft: **Three**
Displacement (full load): **45,923tnes (45,200t)**	Crew: **1793**
Machinery: **Steam Turbines**	Launched: **February 1942**
Armour (belt): **309.88mm (12.2in)**	Speed: **27 knots**

The fourth and last battleship of the "South Dakota" class, the USS *Alabama* (BB60) was launched on 16 February 1942 and completed in August of that year. After a period of working up and convoy protection duty in the Arctic, she and the *South Dakota* arrived at Scapa Flow in June 1943, releasing two British battleships for service in the Mediterranean to cover the Allied landings on Sicily.

The two American battleships then transferred to the Pacific, forming part of Task Group 58.2, and in January 1944 they took part in attacks on Japanese bases in the Marshall Islands. *Alabama* subsequently participated in all the US Navy's main fleet actions in the Pacific, being involved in the Battle of the Philippine Sea and in actions at the Gilbert Islands, Truk, Palau, Saipan, Guam, Luzon, Taiwan, Okinawa and the bombardment of the Japanese home islands. It was a role to which the big battleships were ideally suited, especially as the Americans had almost total supremacy in the air and could give the ships protection.

On 5 June 1945 she was damaged in a typhoon off Okinawa. She was decommissioned in January 1947, but was not stricken until June 1962. She was subsequently transferred to the State of Alabama, to be preserved as a permanent memorial at the naval base of Mobile.

ATLANTA

Launched on 6 September 1941, the USS *Atlanta* was the leader of a class of 11 light anti-aircraft cruisers (the Americans had seen the dangers that enemy aircraft posed to their maritime vessels and fleets). In June 1942 she was in action at the Battle of Midway, and in August she was one of the warships covering the American landing in the island of Guadalcanal, later taking part in the sea and air battle that raged east of the Solomons as US and Japanese forces battled for possession of that strategic position.

In October 1942, as one of the cruisers providing the anti-aircraft screen for Task Force 64, she was present at the Battle of Santa Cruz, and later provided escort to the convoys carrying vital supplies to the US forces on Guadalcanal. On 6 November 1942 she sailed from Espiritu Santu as part of Task Group 62.4, escorting a troop convoy bound for the island. The convoy arrived on the 12th and began the process of disembarking, but this was halted when air reconnaissance reported strong Japanese naval forces approaching. In a series of fierce night engagements the American force was broken up, the *Atlanta* sinking in the early hours of 13 November after receiving gun and torpedo hits. The name *Atlanta* was later assumed by a cruiser of the "Cleveland-Fargo" class, launched in June 1944.

SPECIFICATIONS

ATLANTA

Type: **Antiaircraft Cruiser**	Armour (deck): **30.48mm (1.2in)**
Length: **165.5m (543ft)**	Armour (turrets): **30.48mm (1.2in)**
Beam: **16.55m (54.3ft)**	Guns: **16x5in**
Draught: **6.09m (20ft)**	AA guns: **3x1.1in; 24x40 & 14x20m**
Displacement (normal): **6096tnes (6000t)**	Aircraft: **None**
Displacement (full load): **2591tnes (8500t)**	Crew: **590**
Machinery: **Steam Turbines**	Launched: **September 1941**
Armour (belt): **88.9mm (3.5in)**	Speed: **32.5 knots**

AUGUSTA

SPECIFICATIONS

AUGUSTA

Type: **Heavy Cruiser**	Armour (deck): **76.2mm (3in)**
Length: **182.88m (600ft)**	Armour (turrets): **38.1mm (1.5in)**
Beam: **20.91m (66.25ft)**	Guns: **9x8in; 8x5in**
Draught: **7.01m (23ft)**	AA guns: **32x40mm; 27x20mm**
Displacement (normal): **9195tnes (9050t)**	Aircraft: **Four**
Displacement (full load): **12,497tnes (12,300t)**	Crew: **872**
Machinery: **Geared Turbines**	Launched: **February 1930**
Armour (belt): **76.2mm (3in)**	Speed: **32.7 knots**

A heavy cruiser of the "Northampton" class, the USS *Augusta* (CA31) was launched on 1 February 1930 and was fitted out to perform the role of flagship, as were two others of her class, *Chicago* and *Houston*.

She saw her early war service in the Atlantic, and in November 1942 she was one of the warships covering the Allied Western Task Force, landing troops on the west coast of Morocco as part of Operation Torch, the Allied invasion of North Africa. This was a relatively easy landing, with the enemy having little in the way of aircraft or naval assets.

In July 1943, as part of a plan to divert the Germans' attention from the Mediterranean, where the Allies were about to land on Sicily, she accompanied the US battleships *Alabama* and *South Dakota*, then based at Scapa Flow in the Orkney Islands, as they carried out a feint operation towards the coast of Norway, together with British battleships and aircraft carriers. In June 1944, during the Allied landings in Normandy, she was the flagship of Admiral Kirk, commanding the Western Task Force, and in August she provided fire support during the landing of the 1st Special Force on the island of Levante, off the Mediterranean coast of France. She remained in service after the war, and was finally broken up in 1960.

CHICAGO

Like *Augusta* and *Houson,* the "Northampton"-class heavy cruiser USS *Chicago* was equipped as a flagship, having extra accommodation for an admiral and his battle staff. Like most US ships of the period, she had good armament against enemy aircraft. She was launched on 10 April 1930. On 7 December 1941 she was escorting the aircraft carrier *Lexington,* ferrying aircraft to Midway Island, and so escaped the Japanese attack on Pearl Harbor.

Early in 1942 she formed part of a combined Australian, American and New Zealand naval squadron operating in the southwest Pacific, and was present at the Battle of the Coral Sea in May. In June 1942, the squadron to which Chicago belonged was designated Task Force 44 under Rear-Admiral Crutchley, RN, and in August it formed the Southern Covering Force during the American landings on Guadalcanal.

On the night of 9 August 1942, *Chicago* was badly damaged by torpedoes from Japanese warships passing through the narrows between Savo Island and Guadalcanal. After repair, she was assigned to Task Force 18, escorting supply convoys to Guadalcanal. On 29 January 1943 she was damaged in a heavy torpedo attack by Japanese aircraft, and sunk in a second attack the next day.

SPECIFICATIONS

CHICAGO

Type:	**Heavy Cruiser**	Armour (deck):	**76.2mm (3in)**
Length:	**182.88m (600ft)**	Armour (turrets):	**38.1mm (1.5in)**
Beam:	**20.19m (66.25ft)**	Guns:	**9x8in; 8x5in**
Draught:	**7.01m (23ft)**	AA guns:	**32x40mm; 27x20mm**
Displacement (normal):	**9195tnes (9050t)**	Aircraft:	**Four**
Displacement (full load):	**12,497tnes (12,300t)**	Crew:	**872**
Machinery:	**Geared Turbines**	Launched:	**April 1930**
Armour (belt):	**76.2mm (3in)**	Speed:	**32.7 knots**

DENVER

SPECIFICATIONS

DENVER

Type:
Light Cruiser

Length:
185.31m (608ft)

Beam:
19.35m (63.5ft)

Draught:
6.7m (22ft)

Displacement (normal):
10,160tnes (10,000t)

Displacement (full load):
14,109tnes (13,887t)

Machinery:
Steam Turbines

Armour (belt):
127mm (5in)

Armour (deck):
76.2mm (3in)

Armour (turrets):
127mm (5in)

Guns:
12x6in; 12x5in

AA guns:
8x40mm; 19x20mm

Aircraft:
Three

Crew:
900

Launched:
April 1942

Speed:
33 knots

One of the large "Cleveland-Fargo" class of light cruisers, the USS *Denver* (CL58) was launched on 4 April 1942. For a light vessel she was well armed, and would prove her worth during the Pacific conflict.

She went into action in the South Pacific in March 1943 as part of Task Force 68, bombarding Japanese airfields in New Georgia and participating in an action that resulted in the sinking of two Japanese destroyers. In November 1943, now assigned to Task Force 39, she was one of the warships covering the American landing in Bougainville (part of the Solomon Islands group), and in September–October 1944, with Task Force 31, she lent her fire support to the landings in the Palau group of atolls.

The provision of fire support continued to be *Denver*'s main task throughout the remainder of the Pacific war, from Leyte Gulf in October 1944 through to her final operations, the bombardment of Japanese mainland targets on Southern Honshu in July 1945.

Her bombardment actions in the interim period, covering amphibious landings while attached to various task groups, included Mindoro, Lingayen Gulf, Palawan, Mindanao and Okinawa. *Denver* survived the war despite her many major engagements, and was finally scrapped in November 1960.

DUANE

The United States Coast Guard cutter *Duane* was one of seven vessels in the "Treasury" class, so called because the ships were named after former Secretaries of the Treasury. They were large gunboats, and rendered excellent service on convoy escort duty in World War II, despite their relatively light armament and their small dimensions.

Duane was launched on 3 June 1936. One of the class, the *Alexander Hamilton*, was sunk off Reykjavik by the *U132* on 29 January 1942; the surviving boats were used as convoy flagships during up to 1944, and as amphibious force flagships in 1944–45.

Some of *Duane*'s convoy escort duties took her into the Mediterranean; for example, on 19–20 April 1944 she led a strongly-escorted convoy, UGS38, through the Straits of Gibraltar.

The 87-ship convoy was heavily attacked from the air, two freighters and the destroyer USS *Lansdale* being sunk. During the Allied landings in southern France in August 1944, *Duane* was the flagship of Rear-Admiral Lowry, commanding Task Force 84. The ships reverted to gunboat status and resumed their normal coast guard duties in 1946. Remarkably, *Duane* and four other vessels of the class remained active until the 1980s, giving good service until they were retired.

SPECIFICATIONS

DUANE

Type: **Coast Guard Cutter**	Armour (deck): **None**
Length: **99.66m (327ft)**	Armour (turrets): **N/A**
Beam: **12.49m (41ft)**	Guns: **2x6pdr; 1x1pdr**
Draught: **3.81m (12.5ft)**	AA guns: **None**
Displacement (normal): **2252tnes (2216t)**	Aircraft: **One**
Displacement (full load): **2388tnes (2350t)**	Crew: **123**
Machinery: **Geared Turbines**	Launched: **June 1936**
Armour (belt): **88.9mm (3.5in)**	Speed: **19.5 knots**

ENTERPRISE

SPECIFICATIONS

ENTERPRISE

Type: **Aircraft Carrier**	Armour (deck): **None**
Length: **246.58m (809ft)**	Armour (turrets): **N/A**
Beam: **29.1m (95.5ft)**	Guns: **8x5in; 40x40mm**
Draught: **6.52m (21.4ft)**	AA guns: **16x1.1in; 25x.5in**
Displacement (normal): **20,218tnes (19,900t)**	Aircraft: **100**
Displacement (full load): **25,892tnes (25,484t)**	Crew: **2702**
Machinery: **Geared Turbines**	Launched: **October 1936**
Armour (belt): **101.6mm (4in)**	Speed: **34 knots**

The USS *Enterprise* (CV-6) was a sister vessel of the *Yorktown* and *Hornet* and was a progressive development of the *Ranger* type. She was launched on 3 October 1936 and completed in May 1938, sailing to join the US Pacific Fleet at Pearl Harbor. She was to become one of th emost famous US aircraft carriers to see action in the Pacific.

As the flagship of Task Force 8 under Vice-Admiral Halsey, she was at sea when the Japanese attacked, delivering aircraft to Wake Island. In April 1942 she escorted the USS *Hornet* on the famous Tokyo raid, when *Hornet* flew off B-25 bombers to attack the Japanese capital. During the Battle of Midway *Enterprise*'s torpedo bombers suffered terrible casualties, but her dive bombers and those of her sister ships sank three Japanese carriers, changing the course of the war. On 24 August 1942 *Enterprise* was hit by three bombs during the Battle of the Eastern Solomons, losing 74 dead, and on 26 October she took two bomb hits at the Battle of Santa Cruz, with 44 dead.

She was present at all the US Navy's subsequent Pacific campaigns, surviving two damaging attacks by *kamikazes* off Okinawa in April and May 1945. After the war she served as an attack carrier and as an anti-submarine warfare carrier, and was broken up in 1957.

HEERMAN

The USS *Heermann* (DD532) was one of the very numerous "Fletcher" class destroyers, a highly successful design that became the backbone of the US Pacific Fleet in World War II. In all, 360 were built. *Heermann* was launched on 5 December 1942 and first went into action in November 1943 during Operation Galvanic, the American landings on Tarawa and other islands in the Gilbert group (during which the US ground forces suffered grievous losses). During this operation, she gave fire support to the US 2nd Marine Division, which experienced some of the bitterest fighting of the war on Tarawa. In October 1944 *Heermann* took part in the Battle of Leyte Gulf, and in March 1945 she was part of the large number of warships escorting carriers whose air groups made the first major raid on the Japanese Home Islands. On 17 April 1945 she assisted in the sinking of the Japanese submarine *I-56* off Okinawa.

In the closing weeks of the war, she again formed part of the escort force for aircraft carriers and battleships raiding the Japanese mainland alomst at will, and in August she was at the forefront of Task Force 38, which sailed into Sagami Bay to receive the Japanese surrender. In August 1961 *Heermann* was sold to Argentina as the *Almirante Brown*.

SPECIFICATIONS

HEERMAN

Type: **Destroyer**	Armour (deck): **12.7mm (.5in)**
Length: **114.75m (375.5ft)**	Armour (turrets): **12.7mm (.5in)**
Beam: **12.03m (39.5ft)**	Guns: **5x5in**
Draught: **3.81m (12.5ft)**	AA guns: **6x40mm; 10x20mm**
Displacement (normal): **2173tnes (2050t)**	Aircraft: **None**
Displacement (full load): **2540tnes (2500t)**	Crew: **353**
Machinery: **Steam Turbines**	Launched: **December 1942**
Armour (belt): **19mm (.75in)**	Speed: **36.5 knots**

HORNET

SPECIFICATIONS

HORNET

Type:
Aircraft Carrier

Length:
246.58m (809ft)

Beam:
25.4m (83.34ft)

Draught:
6.52m (21.4ft)

Displacement (normal):
20,218tnes (19,900t)

Displacement (full load):
25,892tnes (25,484t)

Machinery:
Geared Turbines

Armour (belt):
101.6mm (4in)

Armour (deck):
None

Armour (turrets):
N/A

Guns:
8x5in

AA guns:
16x1.1in; 24x40mm

Aircraft:
100

Crew:
2702

Launched:
December 1940

Speed:
34 knots

The third vessel of the "Yorktown" class, the USS *Hornet* (CV-7) differed from her sister ships *Yorktown* and *Enterprise* in having a larger flight deck and two catapults. Laid down at Newport News in September 1939, she was launched on 14 December 1940 and completed in October 1941.

In April 1942 she leapt to fame as the carrier that launched 16 B-25 bombers, led by Lt-Col Jimmy Doolittle, to attack Tokyo. Although the raids did little material damage, they persuaded the Japanese to make further Pacific conquests in order to extend their perimeter. This resulted in over-extended supply lines on which their merchant fleet was decimated by American submarines. *Hornet* saw action at the Battle of Midway, in which her torpedo squadrons suffered heavy casualties, but her dive bombers contributed to the sinking of three Japanese carriers.

In October 1942 she provided escort to convoys resupplying the garrison on Guadalcanal, the scene of fierce fighting. On 26 October 1942, during the Battle of Santa Cruz, *Hornet* was hit by four bombs and two torpedoes, as well as two crashing aircraft, and was again damaged by another torpedo in a second attack. She was abandoned, having lost 111 of her crew, and later sunk by Japanese destroyers.

HOUSTON

The heavy cruiser USS *Houston* (CA30) was one of the six "Northampton" class vessels. Built at Newport News, she was launched on 7 September 1929. In December 1941, as flagship of the American Task Force 5, she was engaged in escort duty in the southwest Pacific, and early in February 1942 she formed part of the Allied naval forces operating off the Dutch East Indies. On 4 February the ships were sighted by a strong force of Japanese bombers, and in the ensuing attack one of *Houston*'s 203mm (8in) gun turrets was blown off (though considering the size of air fleet, she had been lucky not to have been sunk). Despite this damage she was in action later in the month, forming part of the Allied naval force under the command of the Dutch Admiral Karel Doorman.

At the end of March, in what became known as the Battle of Sunda Strait, *Houston* and other warships attempted to intercept Japanese invasion forces landing troops on Java. *Houston* and the Australian cruiser *Perth* managed to sink two large troops transports and damage a destroyer and a minesweeper, but in a fierce gun and torpedo exchange between the Allied warships and enemy cruisers and destroyers, *Houston* and *Perth* were both sunk. The Battle of the Java Sea was a complete disaster for Allied naval power.

SPECIFICATIONS

HOUSTON

Type: **Heavy Cruiser**	Armour (deck): **76.2mm (3in)**
Length: **182.88m (600ft)**	Armour (turrets): **38.1mm (1.5in)**
Beam: **20.19m (66.25ft)**	Guns: **9x8in; 8x5in**
Draught: **7.01m (23ft)**	AA guns: **32x40mm; 27x20mm**
Displacement (normal): **9195tnes (9050t)**	Aircraft: **Four**
Displacement (full load): **12,497tnes (12,300t)**	Crew: **872**
Machinery: **Geared Turbines**	Launched: **September 1929**
Armour (belt): **76.2mm (3in)**	Speed: **32.7 knots**

INDIANAPOLIS

SPECIFICATIONS

INDIANAPOLIS

Type: **Heavy Cruiser**	Armour (deck): **101.6mm (4in)**
Length: **185.92m (610ft)**	Armour (turrets): **63.5mm (2.5in)**
Beam: **20.11m (66ft)**	Guns: **9x8in; 8x5in**
Draught: **6.7m (22ft)**	AA guns: **24x40mm; 28x20mm**
Displacement (normal): **10,008tnes (9850t)**	Aircraft: **Two**
Displacement (full load): **13,970tnes (13,750t)**	Crew: **876**
Machinery: **Geared Turbines**	Launched: **November 1931**
Armour (belt): **127mm (5in)**	Speed: **32.7 knots**

The heavy cruiser USS *Indianapolis* was one of two vessels that were improvements on the "Northampton" class, the other being the USS *Portland*. Launched on 7 November 1931, *Indianapolis* fought her way through the Pacific War from the beginning almost to the very end, when she was lost literally in the last days of hostilities.

Her battle honours included the Coral Sea, Midway, the Eastern Solomons, Santa Cruz, the Gilbert Islands, Kwajalein, Eniwetok, Palau, Leyte Gulf, Midoro Lingayen, Iwo Jima, the Marianas and Okinawa, where she was damaged by a *kamikaze* attack on 30 March 1945. In addition, she took part in numerous raids on Japanese-held islands in the Pacific, 1942–44. She seemed to live a charmed life, but her luck was about to run out.

In July 1945 she transported components of the atomic bombs from San Francisco to Tinian. On the night of 29/30 July, having delivered this vital cargo, she was proceeding to Leyte when she was hit by a salvo of six torpedoes from the Japanese submarine *I-58* and sunk with the loss of all but 316 of her 1199 crew, the survivors being picked up by American flying boats and destroyers between 2 August and 8 August. Many survived the attack, only to fall victim to sharks.

JOHNSTON

The "Fletcher"-class destroyer USS *Johnston* was launched on 25 March 1943. In January 1944 she formed part of Task Force 53 under Rear-Admiral Connolly, which landed the 4th Marine Division on Roi atoll in the Central Pacific, and in July she was part of the escort for Task Group 53.2 under Rear-Admiral Reifsnider, which landed the 1st Marine Brigade and elements of the 77th Infantry Division on Guam.

During the Battle of Leyte in October 1944 she was one of seven destroyers assigned to Rear-Admiral Sprague's Task Unit 3. On 24 October, Sprague's force intercepted a force of Japanese warships attempting to escape to Leyte Gulf through the San Bernadino Strait; torpedoes from the *Johnston* and another destroyer, the *Hoel*, hit the Japanese cruiser *Kumano* and brought her to a standstill. Shortly afterwards, however, the *Johnston* and *Hoel* came under heavy and effective fire from the Japanese battleships *Yamato* and *Nagato* and both were sunk, together with the destroyer *Samuel B. Roberts* and the escort carrier *Gambier Bay*.

The Battle of Leyte Gulf, which witnessed heavy losses on both sides, was the first occasion on which organized *kamikaze* attacks were made. Like many such attacks, their psychological value was greater than the material damage they inflicted.

SPECIFICATIONS

JOHNSTON

Type: **Destroyer**	Armour (deck): **12.7mm (.5in)**
Length: **114.75m (376.5ft)**	Armour (turrets): **12.7mm (.5in)**
Beam: **12.03m (39.5ft)**	Guns: **5x5in**
Draught: **3.81m (12.5ft)**	AA guns: **6x40mm; 10x20mm**
Displacement (normal): **2083tnes (2050t)**	Aircraft: **None**
Displacement (full load): **2540tnes (2500t)**	Crew: **358**
Machinery: **Steam Turbines**	Launched: **March 1943**
Armour (belt): **19mm (.75in)**	Speed: **36.5 knots**

LEXINGTON

SPECIFICATIONS

LEXINGTON

Type: **Aircraft Carrier**	Armour (deck): **76.2mm (3in)**
Length: **270.66m (888ft)**	Armour (turrets): **N/A**
Beam: **32.3m (106ft)**	Guns: **8x8in; 12x5in**
Draught: **7.34m (24.1ft)**	AA guns: **16x1.1in; 16x.5in**
Displacement (normal): **33,528tnes (33,000t)**	Aircraft: **80–90**
Displacement (full load): **44,094tnes (43,400t)**	Crew: **1899**
Machinery: **Express Boilers**	Launched: **October 1925**
Armour (belt): **152.4mm (6in)**	Speed: **33 knots**

America's second aircraft carrier, the USS *Lexington* was originally ordered as a battlecruiser named *Constitution*, but was renamed *Lexington* in December 1917. In July 1922 she was re-ordered as an aircraft carrier (CV-2) and launched on 3 October 1925. She appeared in US Fleet exercises for the first time in January 1929, together with her sister ship *Saratoga* (CV-3). In December 1929, she made headlines when she served as a floating power plant for the city of Tacoma, Washington, following a massive power failure. Her career during World War II was to prove that aircraft carriers, now the caital ships of the fleet, could also be vulnerable to enemy aircraft.

After the Japanese attack on Pearl Harbor her air group was involved in the battle for Wake Island, followed by convoy escort duty. In May 1942 she was operating as part of Task Force 11, a joint Allied naval force formed to prevent a Japanese landing at Port Moresby, New Guinea. In the Battle of the Coral Sea, which began in the morning of 8 May 1942 after the opposing carrier task forces sighted one another and launched their respective strike forces, *Lexington* was hit by two torpedoes and three bombs and had to be abandoned, being sunk later by the destroyer USS *Phelps*. Casualties included 216 dead.

MARYLAND

The battleship USS *Maryland* (BB46) was one of a class of four, the others being the *Colorado*, *Washington* and *West Virginia*. They were built in response to a new Japanese naval construction programme, although *Washington* was not completed in order to comply with the terms of the Washington Naval Treaty. *Maryland* was launched on 20 March 1920 and completed in July 1921, joining the US Pacific Fleet in the following year.

On 7 December 1941 she was damaged in the Japanese attack on Pearl Harbor (being one of the vessels neatly lined up for the Japanese aircraft that attacked the base), and while she was undergoing repair at Bremerton her anti-aircraft armament was increased, among other improvements. This turned her into a powerful vessel.

On 22 June 1944, off Saipan, she was damaged by an aircraft torpedo which hit her in the bow, and was again damaged in a *kamikaze* attack off Leyte on 29 November, 31 crew members being killed. During the subsequent repair and refit she underwent further modification, including the replacement of her secondary armament. On 7 April 1945 she was seriously damaged by a *kamikaze* off Okinawa, effectively putting her out of the war. She was decommissioned in 1947 and broken up in 1959.

SPECIFICATIONS

MARYLAND

Type: **Battleship**	*Armour (deck):* **88.9mm (3.5in)**
Length: **190.34m (624.5ft)**	*Armour (turrets):* **457.2mm (18in)**
Beam: **29.71m (97.5ft)**	*Guns:* **8x16in; 12x5in; 4x3in**
Draught: **10.69m (35.1ft)**	*AA guns:* **8x.5in**
Displacement (normal): **33,020tnes (32,500t)**	*Aircraft:* **None**
Displacement (full load): **38,100tnes (37,500t)**	*Crew:* **1500**
Machinery: **Geared Turbines**	*Launched:* **March 1920**
Armour (belt): **342.9m (13.5in)**	*Speed:* **21 knots**

MISSOURI

SPECIFICATIONS

MISSOURI

Type:
Battleship

Length:
270.35m (887ft)

Beam:
32.91m (108ft)

Draught:
11.27m (37ft)

Displacement (normal):
45,720tnes (45,000t)

Displacement (full load):
60,280tnes (59,331t)

Machinery:
Geared Turbines

Armour (belt):
309.88mm (12.2in)

Armour (deck):
127mm (5in)

Armour (turrets):
431.8mm (17in)

Guns:
9x16in; 20x5in

AA guns:
80x40mm; 60x20mm

Aircraft:
Three

Crew:
1851

Launched:
January 1944

Speed:
33 knots

The USS *Missouri* (BB-63) was one of six "Iowa"-class battleships, two of which (*Illinois* and *Kentucky*) were not completed. They were the fastest battleships ever built, with a high length to beam ratio. *Missouri* was launched on 29 January 1944 and completed in June of that year. She joined the Pacific Fleet in time to take part in the first major carrier air raids on the Japanese mainland in March 1945, forming part of the escort force. In many ways these ships were the ultimate in batttleship design, but were obsolete even before they left the shipyard.

On 24 March, together with the battleships *Wisconsin* and *New Jersey*, she shelled the island of Okinawa as part of the softening-up operation prior to the American landing. During the landing phase of the operation, on 11 April 1945, she was damaged by a *kamikaze*, and she received moderate damage in another *kamikaze* attack on 16 April. In July she joined other capital ships in bombarding the Japanese mainland, and on 27 August she was part of the 3rd Fleet, sailing into Sagami Bay to accept the Japanese surrender, which was signed on board. *Missouri* carried out shore bombardment during the Korean War and also during the Gulf War, having been rearmed with cruise missiles. She is now a permanent memorial at Pearl Harbor.

PITTSBURGH

The heavy cruiser USS *Pittsburgh* (CA72), formerly named *Albany*, was launched on 22 February 1944. She was one of 24 planned vessels of the "Baltimore" class, and she went into action with the Pacific Fleet in March 1944, sailing from the anchorage at Ulithi Atoll as part of Admiral Mitscher's Task Force 58 to escort aircraft carriers making an attack on the Japanese Home Islands. During this action she and the cruiser *Santa Fe* rescued 1700 survivors from the aircraft carriers *Wasp* and *Franklin*, both heavily damaged by Japanese bombers (*Franklin* had 724 men killed and 265 injured).

In April 1945 *Pittsburgh* was attached to Task Group 58.2, supporting the landings on Okinawa. On 5 June, together with many other US warships, *Pittsburgh* was badly damaged in a typhoon, having 10.6m (35ft) of her bows torn away. However, her design meant she was able to withstand such damage. And it also gave the class long service life.

After repair *Pittsburgh* was returned to active duty and remained in service for many years after the war, being stricken in 1973. Of the original 24 vessels of the "Baltimore" class laid down, six were cancelled in August 1945 with the end of the war in the Pacific. Some, including *Pittsburgh*, were extensively modernized in the 1960s.

SPECIFICATIONS

PITTSBURGH

Type: **Heavy Cruiser**	*Armour (deck):* **65mm (2.56mm)**
Length: **205.13m (673ft)**	*Armour (turrets):* **211.32mm (8.32in)**
Beam: **21.25m (69.75ft)**	*Guns:* **9x8in; 12x5in**
Draught: **6.55m (21.5ft)**	*AA guns:* **48x40mm; 26x20mm**
Displacement (normal): **13,838tnes (13,620t)**	*Aircraft:* **Four**
Displacement (full load): **17,475tnes (17,200t)**	*Crew:* **1200**
Machinery: **Steam Turbines**	*Launched:* **February 1944**
Armour (belt): **154.43mm (6.08in)**	*Speed:* **33 knots**

RANGER

SPECIFICATIONS

RANGER

Type: **Aircraft Carrier**	Armour (deck): **25.4mm (1in)**
Length: **234.39m (769ft)**	Armour (turrets): **N/A**
Beam: **24.44m (80.2ft)**	Guns: **8x5in**
Draught: **5.94m (19.5ft)**	AA guns: **16x1.1in; 16x.5in**
Displacement (normal): **14,732tnes (14,500t)**	Aircraft: **70**
Displacement (full load): **18,288tnes (18,000t)**	Crew: **1788**
Machinery: **Geared Turbines**	Launched: **February 1933**
Armour (belt): **25.4mm (1in)**	Speed: **30.36 knots**

The only large carrier in the Atlantic Fleet, *Ranger* led the task force that provided air superiority during the amphibious invasion of French Morocco on 8 November 1942, launching 496 combat sorties in the three-day operation. Following training in Chesapeake Bay, the carrier underwent overhaul in the Norfolk Navy Yard from 16 December 1942 to 7 February 1943. She next transported 75 P-40-L army aircraft to Africa, arriving at Casablanca on 23 February; then patrolled and trained pilots along the New England coast. Departing Halifax on 11 August, she joined the British Home Fleet at Scapa Flow on 19 August.

Ranger departed Scapa Flow with the Home Fleet on 2 October to attack German shipping in Norwegian waters. Her aircraft severely damaged a German tanker, a small troop transport, four small merchantmen, a freighter and a small coaster. She did not sustain any damage during this period.

Ranger returned to Scapa Flow on 6 October 1943, and patrolled with the British Second Battle Squadron until the end of the year. In 1944 she was used for training and then underwent a major refit. Operating out of San Diego, she continued training air groups and squadrons along the peaceful California coast for the rest of the war.

SARATOGA

The USS *Saratoga* (CV-3), sister ship to the *Lexington*, was originally laid down as a battlecruiser in 1920. She was reordered as an aircraft carrier in July 1922, when she was one-third complete, and launched on 7 April 1925. Completed in 1928, she joined the Pacific Fleet in the following year. At the time of the Japanese attack on Pearl Harbor she was transporting fighters to Wake Island and consequently escaped, but on 11 January 1942 she was torpedoed by the Japanese submarine *I-6* 800km (500 miles) southwest of Oahu. Her damage was not major, though.

After repair, in June 1942, she joined Admiral Fitch's Task Force 11, but in August she was again torpedoed, this time by the *I-26*. After further repairs she subsequently operated off Guadalcanal. She provided valuable air cover for US ships operating in the area, as well as flying sorties against the enemy.

Her battle honours included the Battle of the Eastern Solomons, the Rabaul raids, the Gilbert Islands, Kwajalein and Eniwetok; she also served with the British Eastern Fleet in the Indian Ocean in 1944, her air group participating in attacks on Sabang. On 21 February 1945 she was severely damaged when hit by four *kamikazes*, putting her out of the war. On 25 July 1946, her hulk was destroyed in the atomic tests at Bikini.

SPECIFICATIONS

SARATOGA

Type: **Aircraft Carrier**	Armour (deck): **76.2mm (3in)**
Length: **270.66m (888ft)**	Armour (turrets): **N/A**
Beam: **32.3m (106ft)**	Guns: **8x8in; 18x5in; 12x5in**
Draught: **7.34m (24.1ft)**	AA guns: **16x1.1in; 30x20mm**
Displacement (normal): **33,528tnes (33,000t)**	Aircraft: **80–90**
Displacement (full load): **44,094tnes (43,400t)**	Crew: **1890**
Machinery: **Electric Turbines**	Launched: **April 1925**
Armour (belt): **152.4mm (6in)**	Speed: **33 knots**

SOUTH DAKOTA

SPECIFICATIONS

SOUTH DAKOTA

Type: **Battleship**	Armour (deck): **38.1mm (1.5in)**
Length: **207.26m (680ft)**	Armour (turrets): **457.2mm (18in)**
Beam: **32.91m (108ft)**	Guns: **9x16in; 20x5in**
Draught: **11.06m (36.3ft)**	AA guns: **24x40mm; 35x20mm**
Displacement (normal): **35,116tnes (34,563t)**	Aircraft: **None**
Displacement (full load): **46,957tnes (46,218t)**	Crew: **1793**
Machinery: **Geared Turbines**	Launched: **June 1941**
Armour (belt): **309.88mm (12.2in)**	Speed: **27.8 knots**

The USS *South Dakota* (BB-57) – the largest of the four vessels in the above potograph – was leader of a class of four battleships, the others being *Alabama, Indiana* and *Massachusetts*. Built at the New York Shipyard, she was launched on 7 June 1941 and completed in March the following year. She was one of the great US battleships of the war.

In September 1942 she suffered hull damage when she struck an uncharted rock in the Tonga Islands, but was repaired in time to see action at the Battle of Santa Cruz, being damaged by a bomb hit in 'A' turret on 26 October. A week later she suffered further damage in a collision with the destroyer *Mahan*, and was again damaged by gunfire on 15 November at the Battle of Guadalcanal, suffering 38 dead.

After this somewhat unfortunate start she went on to acquire an impressive number of battle honours in the Pacific War, taking part in all the US Navy's major operations. She suffered two further mishaps, being hit by a bomb off Saipan on 19 June 1944 with the loss of 27 members of her crew, and damaged by a powder explosion in one of her gun turrets on 6 May 1945. She was present at the Japanese surrender in Sagami Bay on 2 September. *South Dakota* was decommissioned in January 1947 and broken up in 1962.

TEXAS

The USS *Texas* (BB-35) was a Dreadnought-type battleship of the "New York" class, laid down in 1911. She was launched on 18 May 1912 and completed in March 1914. During World War I she was attached to the Royal Navy's Grand Fleet for convoy protection duty in the North Atlantic, operating from Scapa Flow naval base in the Orkneys, and while she was in British waters she became the first US battleship to be fitted with a flying-off platform for spotter aircraft.

From 1919 to 1925 she served with the Pacific Fleet, rejoining the Atlantic Fleet in 1927 after undergoing a period of reconstruction. During World War II, by which time she was obsolete, she again served on convoy protection duty in the Atlantic, and provided fire support for the landings in North Africa in November 1942 and for the D-Day landings in Normandy, June 1944.

During the latter operations, she was damaged by gunfire from a shore battery at Cherbourg. After supporting the Allied landings in the south of France in August 1944 she was transferred to the Pacific, where she provided gunfire support for the American landings on the islands of Iwo Jima and Okinawa. *Texas* was stricken in April 1948 and preserved as a memorial at Galveston, Texas.

SPECIFICATIONS

TEXAS

Type: **Dreadnought**	Armour (deck): **63.5mm (2.5in)**
Length: **174.65m (573ft)**	Armour (turrets): **355.6mm (14in)**
Beam: **29.62m (97.2ft)**	Guns: **10x14in; 37x5in**
Draught: **9.6m (31.5ft)**	AA guns: **8x3in; 8x.5in**
Displacement (normal): **24,432tnes (27,000t)**	Aircraft: **None**
Displacement (full load): **28,956tnes (28,500t)**	Crew: **1054**
Machinery: **Boilers**	Launched: **May 1912**
Armour (belt): **304.8mm (12in)**	Speed: **21 knots**

TUSCALOOSA

SPECIFICATIONS

TUSCALOOSA

Type: **Heavy Cruiser**	Armour (deck): **127mm (5in)**
Length: **179.22m (588ft)**	Armour (turrets): **152.4mm (6in)**
Beam: **18.66m (61.25ft)**	Guns: **9x8in; 8x5in**
Draught: **7.01m (23ft)**	AA guns: **16x40mm; 19x20mm**
Displacement (normal): **10,109tnes (9950t)**	Aircraft: **Four**
Displacement (full load): **13,411tnes (13,200t)**	Crew: **876**
Machinery: **Geared Turbines**	Launched: **November 1933**
Armour (belt): **127mm (5in)**	Speed: **30 knots**

A "New Orleans"-class heavy cruiser, the USS *Tuscaloosa* (CA37) was launched on 15 November 1933. In the early months of World War II she took part in the US patrols in the Atlantic, ranging from Bermuda to the Denmark Strait, and from November 1941 she joined with heavy units of the Royal Navy to counter the expected breakout of the German battleship *Tirpitz* into the North Atlantic (which in the event never happened). In the summer of 1942 she escorted Arctic convoys to Russia, and in November she was one of the warships covering the Allied landings in North Africa, which were relatively easy.

In October 1943 she formed part of an Anglo-American naval force that landed Norwegian troops on the island of Spitzbergen, and later took part in raids on the Norwegian coast.

During the Normandy landings she supported the assault on "Utah" Beach, and in August covered the landings on the French Riviera. At the end of 1944 she was transferred to the Pacific Theatre, where she lent fire support to the American landings on Iwo Jima and Okinawa. *Tuscaloosa* was scrapped at Baltimore in 1959. Three of this class, *Astoria, Quincy* and *Vincennes,* were sunk in a cruiser battle off Guadalcanal on 9 August 1942.

YORKTOWN

The aircraft carrier USS *Yorktown* (CV-5) was launched on 4 April 1936 and completed in September of the following year. Her early service was with the Pacific Fleet, but in June 1941 she was transferred to the Atlantic for convoy protection duty. Her stay in this theatre of war was relatively short-lived, as she returned to the Pacific to form the nucleus of Task Force 17 in time to take part in raids on Japanese-held islands in the Central Pacific in January-February 1942. She was one of the greatest aircraft carriers of the war.

In March her air group was in action against Japanese forces landing in New Guinea, and in May she saw action at the Battle of the Coral Sea, being damaged by enemy bombs. She returned to Pearl Harbor, where repairs were made in only 48 hours, and on 28 May she sailed to intercept Japanese naval forces approaching Midway Island. During the ensuing battle, although her torpedo squadrons suffered heavily, her dive-bomber units contributed to the destruction of three Japanese aircraft carriers and therefore helped to tilt the war in the Pacific in the Americans' favour. However, aircraft from the carrier *Hiryu* hit *Yorktown* with two torpedoes and three bombs on 5 June 1942. Desperate attempts were made to save her, but she was sunk by the submarine *I-168* two days later.

SPECIFICATIONS

YORKTOWN

Type: **Aircraft Carrier**	Armour (deck): **None**
Length: **246.73m (809.5ft)**	Armour (turrets): **N/A**
Beam: **25.4m (83.34ft)**	Guns: **8x5in**
Draught: **6.52m (21.4ft)**	AA guns: **16x1.1in; 24x.5in**
Displacement (normal): **20,218tnes (19,900t)**	Aircraft: **100**
Displacement (full load): **25,892tnes (25,484t)**	Crew: **2702**
Machinery: **Geared Turbines**	Launched: **April 1936**
Armour (belt): **101.6mm (4in)**	Speed: **34 knots**

INDEX